14 Things Witches Hope Parents Never Find Out

David Benoit

All scripture references are from the King James Version unless otherwise stated.

All line drawings by Eric Ferguson.

14 THINGS WITCHES HOPE PARENTS NEVER FIND OUT
Copyright © 1994 by David Benoit
Charlotte, North Carolina

Printed in the United States of America

Published by:
Hearthstone Publishing, Ltd.
901 N.W. 6th Street
Oklahoma City, OK 73106
(405) 235-5396 ● (800) 652-1144
FAX (405) 236-4634

ISBN 1-879366-75-4

Dedication

I would like to dedicate this book to my wife, Debbie, and my children, Brandon and Lindsay, as well as my staff whose hard work made this project a reality.

Table of Contents

Preface

As a parent or grandparent it is becoming extremely hard to rear a "Cleaver family" in a "Bart Simpson society." When the images for our children are violent, sensual, and godless, the pressure is really put on the home.

For many years, parents have felt that the church and Christian school movement was the salvation of their children. Because of my research in rock music, occultism, and witchcraft, I am invited to address Christian school conventions. In my opening remarks I usually say, "I believe in Christian education, but the devil homeschools!" We can teach math, science, English, and even the Bible, but if your child's heroes are rock musicians and those who dabble with the occult via television and radio, the teacher's influence is all but nullified.

A man once said, *"The church cannot raise what the home has put to death."*

The desire of this author is to help you as a parent, grandparent, or friend to identify Satan's devices as he intrudes into your home. People in America invest huge amounts of money to keep intruders on the outside of their homes. Yet through carelessness or lack of knowledge, they freely open their homes to entertainers and those involved in witchcraft who can spiritually and sometimes even physically seduce their children.

I trust the things you will learn from this book, *14 Things Witches Hope Parents Never Find Out*, will work as a warning system to you and your children.

Introduction

For years, witchcraft has been seasonable. It seems every September and October witches are on bulletin boards, front porches, and windows as decorations for the upcoming Halloween season.

But I have news for you. Witchcraft is not just for Halloween anymore. Our children are prime targets of these beliefs. Three hundred and sixty-five days a year, children are being preyed upon by witchcraft through promotion of cartoons, toys, and games, as well as professing witches in the field of education. This puts our children in a very vulnerable position.

It has been said, *"Those who control the youth, control the future."* Could there be a plan in witchcraft to control the future of your child? Does God promise to protect Christian homes when parents allow occult items in their homes? No.

Through this book, you will read some alarming evidence. Some of the information contained in this book includes:

- Understanding which witch is which
- Is there a difference in white and black magic?
- Are trolls, Smurfs, mermaids, Teenage Mutant Ninja Turtles, and other cartoons and games safe for your children?
- Fourteen secrets witches hope parents never find out
- Seven practical ways to prevent your child from getting involved in witchcraft
- Twenty-seven scriptural admonitions for protecting your children

---

Chapter One

God Will Not Protect Children When Parents Allow Occult Items In Their Homes

HI! MY NAME IS MARY, I'M WITH THE CHURCH OF WICCA... IF YOU EVER NEED A BABYSITTER, GIVE ME A CALL.

"Because of the multitude of the whoredoms of the well-favoured harlot, the mistress of witchcrafts, that selleth nations through her whoredoms, and families through her witchcrafts." **(Nahum 3:4)**

There Is No Scriptural Evidence That God Will Protect a Child When Parents Allow Occultic Objects In Their Homes.

Let me begin by saying that this chapter is not to debate philosophical ideas about the innocence of children. This chapter is not to show God as a tyrant against little children. Rather, it is a warning to unsuspecting parents.

What does the Bible say about bringing abominations into your home? Deuteronomy 7:25–26 says: *"The graven images of their gods shall ye burn with fire: thou shalt not desire the silver or gold that is on them, nor take it unto thee, lest thou be snared therein: for it is an abomination to the Lord thy God. Neither shalt thou bring an abomination into thine house, lest thou be a cursed thing like it: but thou shalt utterly detest it, and thou shalt utterly abhor it; for it is a cursed thing."*

When children and teenagers are bringing trolls to Christian schools and churches, bus captains give Smurfs to kids for bus promotions, a pastor's son has the entire set of "Masters of the Universe," and *The Little Mermaid* is shown in children's church, it is time to realize God is serious about bringing abominations into Christian homes and churches.

Does God Hold Children Accountable for Their Parents Actions?

One example is the warning given to God's people not to take the accursed things into Jericho. In Joshua 6:17–18 we read: *"And the city shall be accursed, even it, and all that are therein, to the Lord: only Rahab the harlot shall live, she and all that are with her in the house, because she hid the messengers that we sent. And ye, in any wise keep yourselves from the accursed thing, lest ye make yourselves accursed, when ye take of the accursed thing, and make the camp of Israel a curse, and trouble it."*

Not only did God say the accursed things would affect the home, but the accursed things would also affect the nation. The execution and judgment of God is a terrible thing. Joshua 7:24–25 says, *"And Joshua, and all Israel with him, took Achan the son of Zerah, and the silver, and the garment, and the wedge of gold, and his sons, and his daughters, and his oxen, and his asses, and his sheep, and his tent, and all that he had: and they brought them unto the valley of Achor. And Joshua said, Why hast thou troubled us? the LORD shall trouble thee this day. And all Israel stoned him with stones, and burned them with fire, after they had stoned them with stones."*

We do not know how young Achan's sons and daughters were, but God still had them stoned. God does not tolerate idols and accursed things, even in the home of His children. Although I do not know when a child reaches the age of accountability, I have heard of demon possession in very young children.

A second example is shown in Mark 9:17–29 which says, *"And one of the multitude answered and said, Master, I have brought unto thee my son, which hath a dumb spirit; And wheresoever he taketh him, he teareth him; and he foameth, and gnasheth with his teeth, and pineth away: and I spake to thy disciples that they should cast him out; and they could not. He answereth him, and saith, O faithless generation, how long shall I be with you? how long shall I suffer you? bring him unto me. And they brought him unto him: and when he saw him, straightway the spirit tare him; and he fell on the ground, and wallowed foaming. And he asked his father, How long is it ago since this came unto him? And he said, Of a child. And ofttimes it hath cast him into the fire, and into the waters, to destroy him: but if thou canst do any thing, have compassion on us, and help us. Jesus said unto him, If thou canst believe, all things are possible to him that believeth. And straightway the father of the child cried out, and said with tears, Lord, I believe; help thou mine unbelief. When Jesus saw that the people came running together, he rebuked the foul spirit, saying unto him, Thou dumb and deaf spirit, I charge thee, come out of him, and enter no more into him. And the spirit cried, and rent him sore, and came out of him: and he was as one dead; insomuch that many said, He is dead. But Jesus took him by the hand, and lifted him up; and he arose. And when he was come into the house, his disciples asked him privately, Why could not we cast him out? And he said unto them, This kind can come forth by nothing, but by prayer and fasting."*

Recently I talked with a lady who has a ministry of deliverance. She was asked to talk to a boy who was having problems with demonic activity in his life. When she tried to get the boy to call on the name of Jesus Christ, he just could not do it. Yet, when she said that Jesus created the universe, a man's voice came out of the boy and said, "He-Man is the master of the universe." The boy was only three years old.

CAN CHRISTIAN CHILDREN BE AFFECTED BY DEMONIC ACTIVITY?

Sometime ago, I was in Birmingham, Alabama, speaking for a large church ministry. On Monday morning I was approached by a fifth grade teacher and one of her students. I was running late to get to a radio program, but I could not deny this teacher and her teary-eyed student. The little girl was sobbing as she told me how she had befriended the daughter of a professing witch. This ten-year-old girl came from a Christian home and attended a Christian church. Yet she was having paranormal activity in her bedroom (by paranormal, I mean demonic activity). She told me that she would turn her radio to a Christian station before going to bed, but when she woke up in the morning, it would be on a rock station. Sometimes the television set in her bedroom would turn on by itself in the middle of the night. She would wake up to find that programs she was not permitted to watch would be on her set. Although I did not ask, I am sure that her parents had premium cable channels coming into their home. I prayed for that girl to be delivered from this demonic activity.

There are literally hundreds of stories of children who have paranormal activity in their bedrooms. Do you know why? Because parents have allowed things to be brought into the home that are accursed. God warns us not to bring these things into our homes.

There are two things that you can do with what you have just read. First, you can dismiss it by saying that I am just overreacting, or that I am using scare tactics on you. The Bible says that *"For God hath not given us the spirit of fear; but of power, and of love, and of a sound mind"* (2 Tim. 1:7). Do you realize that fear was the first emotion that Satan used to turn man away from God? In Genesis 3:9–10 we read, *"And the LORD God called unto Adam, and said unto him, Where art thou? And he said, I heard thy voice in the garden, and I was afraid, because I was naked; and I hid myself."* Satan tried to convince Adam that God no longer loved him. Not only does God love us, but He warns us about dangerous things in our lives.

God also says in Isaiah 5:20, *"Woe unto them that call evil good, and good evil; that put darkness for light, and light for darkness; that put bitter for sweet, and sweet for bitter!"* The Bible says that we should never call good evil, or evil good. You live very dangerously when you say that which is evil is good—like trolls, wizards, and sorcerers. I love my children, as I'm sure that you love yours, and I would not want to put anything in front of them that might harm them in any way.

Secondly, you can consider this and make a logical and biblical decision about what to do. God also promises to give you a sound mind, which means that you will be able to make wise decisions. God's Word is simple to understand, but many times we try to make it difficult. Does God mean what He says when He tells us not to bring the accursed thing into our home?

In conclusion, if you are right about these things just being a toy or game, then your children are okay. But, if I am right, and God does look at them as being an accursed thing, then you are putting your children in a very dangerous situation.

Chapter Two

Understanding Which Witch Is Which

HONEY, I'M SO PROUD OF YOU, SOMEDAY YOU'LL GROW UP TO BE JUST LIKE ME ...

"Ye shall know them by their fruits. Do men gather grapes of thorns, or figs of thistles? Even so every good tree bringeth forth good fruit; but a corrupt tree bringeth forth evil fruit. A good tree cannot bring forth evil fruit, neither can a corrupt tree bring forth good fruit." (Matt. 7:16–18)

They have their own television programs. They have their own churches. They are recognized by the military as a bona fide religion. Our government grants them non-profit status. When Michael Dukakis was running for president of the United States of America, he honored Laurie Cabot as the official one of Salem. They are given the opportunity to lecture on public educational campuses across our nation. It has been estimated that over one hundred and fifty thousand openly profess it as their religion (this is a very low estimate). They are doctors, lawyers, teachers, librarians, and Wall Street executives. They are actors and actresses. These common, everyday people are just like you and me. Or are they? These people belong to a religion called *Wicca*, but you know them better as simply witches.

Let's talk about this religion. The word *wicca* can mean "wise one," "prophet," or "sorcerer." By dissecting this definition, we can learn a little about their religion. First, let's look at "wise one." Why are they called "wise ones"? The answer may lie in the definition of the occult. The word *occult* means "hidden things." Those involved with Wicca may believe they are "wise ones," because they have found the hidden knowledge of the occult. Satan has always tried to convince man that God is holding out on him.

Genesis 3:3 says, *"But of the fruit of the tree which is in the midst of the garden, God hath said, Ye shall not eat of it, neither shall ye touch it, lest ye die."*

ARE "WISE ONES" MENTIONED IN THE SCRIPTURE ASSOCIATED WITH DEMONISM?

Exodus 7:10–13 says, *"And Moses and Aaron went in unto Pharaoh, and they did so as the LORD had commanded: and Aaron cast down his rod before Pharaoh, and before his servants, and it became a serpent. Then Pharaoh also called the wise men and the sorcerers: now the magicians of Egypt, they also did in like manner with their enchantments. For they cast down every man his rod, and they became serpents: but Aaron's rod swallowed up their rods. And he hardened Pharaoh's heart, that he hearkened not unto them; as the Lord had said."* (Before you tell your children that supernatural magic is just make-believe, you had better read the Bible. I find most parents fall into Satan's trap by not knowing what is make-believe and what is real.)

As always, people involved in witchcraft or sorcery were used of Satan to harden the heart of man against God. At first, we looked at the word "seer" or "wise one." Now, let's look at the word *prophet*.

HOW CAN THEY TELL THE FUTURE IF THEY ARE NOT OF GOD?

Deuteronomy 13:1–3 says, *"If there arise among you a prophet, or a dreamer of dreams, and giveth thee a sign or a wonder, And the sign or the wonder come to pass, whereof he spake unto thee, saying, Let us go after other gods, which thou hast not known, and let us serve them; Thou shalt not hearken unto the words of that prophet, or that dreamer of dreams: for the LORD your God proveth you, to know whether ye love the LORD your God with all your heart and with all your soul."*

The devil does not know all the details of the future. Although he cannot accurately predict the future, if he is allowed to he can manipulate the future. For example, a psychic may tell you that you are going to have a wreck with a red car. Satan may know that there is a person in your neighborhood with a red car that he can control. He may control that person, but he cannot control your future.

I remember a woman in one of my services telling me that her sister had played with a Ouija board. The board told her sister that she was going to die. It even told her the date that she would die, as well as how it would happen. She was told that on a certain date her husband would kill her. This disbelieving woman laughed at the very thought of her husband killing her. Strangely enough, on the very date that the board told her it would happen, her husband walked into her bedroom and shot her. The Ouija board is not a toy. It is classified as a mode of communication with spirits.

"Ouija board: A popular form of divination in which people seek spiritualistic or telepathic messages. A number of people have tested the Ouija board by asking about Jesus Christ and the cross. The board's dramatic responses, ranging from violent shaking to flipping against a wall or person, demonstrate demonic hatred of Christ."[1]

WHAT IS THE TRUE TEST OF A REAL PROPHET?

Deuteronomy 18:20–22 says, *"But the prophet, which shall presume to speak a word in my name, which I have not commanded him to speak, or that shall speak in the name of other gods, even that prophet shall die. And if thou say in thine heart, How shall we know the word which the LORD hath not spoken? When a prophet speaketh in the name of the LORD, if the thing follow not, nor come to pass, that is the thing which the LORD hath not spoken, but the prophet hath spoken it presumptuously: thou shalt not be afraid of him."*

The true test of a prophet is that he must be one hundred percent accurate. It doesn't matter if it is a psychic or a television preacher who says, "Thus says the Lord." If the prophecy doesn't come to pass, that person is a false prophet. He is not of God. Did you hear about the psychic fair? According to an AP report of Saturday, January 26, 1991, seven self-styled psychics were arrested in Independence, Missouri. Sergeant David Smith said, *"We consider these readings a fraud. If they can tell the future, how come they didn't know we were coming?"2*

Jeane Dixon has made a lot of predictions. Nostradamus made many predictions. These are supposedly the best psychics of all time. But, if they missed only one prediction, according to the Bible that prophet should die.

SHOULD WE BE AFRAID OF THESE WITCHES AND SEERS?

The Bible says we should not be afraid. What about sorcerers? The word *sorcerer* is derived from the Greek word *pharmakeia*. It is the word from which we get "pharmacy," or drugs. And while not all witches use drugs, some do. One thing that drugs are able to do is alter the state of consciousness. Some witches and occultists do not need drugs to alter their state of consciousness; they can do it directly through demonic spirits.

Did you know that commercial sorcery is mentioned in prophecy? In Revelation 18:23 we read, *". . . for thy merchants were the great men of the earth; for by thy sorceries were all nations deceived."* This is a prediction that great men of the earth used their sorceries to deceive the nations. So, when you give your children toys of demonic origin and tell them that it is just make-believe, you are contributing to an industry that will deceive the nations.

What does deceive mean? It means to be misrepresented. When parents buy wizards, trolls, unicorns, and witches for make-believe, children and parents are deceived. Let me show you how powerfully this fantasy and make-believe sorcery will be used during the Tribulation period.

Revelation 9:20–21 says, *"And the rest of the men which were not killed by these plagues yet repented not of the works of their hands, that they should not worship devils, and idols of gold, and silver, and brass, and stone, and of wood: which neither can see, nor hear, nor walk: Neither repented they of their murders, nor of their sorceries, nor of their fornication, nor of their thefts."* What were the things they would not give up? They would not give up their idols of gold, silver, brass, and wood. The reason they may not have wanted to give up these inanimate objects is that they believed that the objects had protective qualities.

Those involved in witchcraft, demonism, and Satanism have several objects that they use for protection.

1. **Amulet**—an ornament or charm supposedly charged with magical power and used to ward off spells, demons, and bad luck.
2. **Charms**—chanted or spoken words used to invoke a spell or an object said to have supernatural power.
3. **Talisman**—used for protection because they have magical powers, like a sorcerer's wand.

When will these sorceries come to an end? According to Revelation 21:8, those who practice sorcery will have their place in the lake of fire.

The title of this chapter is "Understanding Which Witch Is Which." Today, people are constantly hearing that witches are just misunderstood people. The one thing I don't understand is why every witch ever interviewed is a "good witch." I hear that there are two types of witches: those who practice "white" magic, and those who practice "black" magic. But only those who practice "white" magic are ever heard from. Usually when they say they are into evil, they are into voodoo or Satanism, but they don't call themselves "black" witches. Could it possibly be that there is no such thing as witches who practice "black" magic? Or are they the same?

Chapter Three

Witches In White Magic and People In Demonism Have Some Things In Common

"BUT PASTOR WILLIAMS! WITCHES DON'T BELIEVE IN SILLY THINGS AS DEMONS!"

"For we wrestle not against flesh and blood, but against principalities, against powers, against the rulers of the darkness of this world, against spiritual wickedness in high places." (Eph. 6:12)

I was doing a live radio talk show when an irate male witch called in over the fact that I had lumped good witches with bad witches. He claimed that he was a good witch and he was offended. I asked him, "What makes you a good witch?"

He quickly replied, "I do good things for people."

To which I replied, "Suppose I made you very angry. Could you curse me?"

His response was, "Yes, of course I could."

He soon found himself trapped with his own words. If a person can admit that a good witch does good things, and a bad witch does evil things, what do you call a person who does both? The answer is a witch.

> *"Magic is variously described as white, black, and gray, but actually it has no color. Magic is neutral and amoral. It can be bent to good, evil, or ambiguous purposes, depending on the intent of the practitioner. The distinction between 'white' and 'black' magic is fairly modern, according to occultist A.E. Waite. It depends upon sharp contrasts between good and evil spirits. The distinctions were far more obscure in ancient times."*[3]

Let's take a look at the difference between "white" magic and "black" magic.

WHITE MAGIC

People who practice "white" magic say that they get their powers from elemental spirits. (If your children watch *Captain Planet*, they will know at least four of the five elemental spirits—earth, wind, fire, water, and spirit.)

According to *Man, Myth, and Magic*, "white" magic is known as "ancestral science," and also as the art of compulsion of the supernatural.[1] Magic is in practice, a human technique, designed to control the environment. It is based on the belief that the forces of nature can be recruited to serve man's interests.

BLACK MAGIC

On the other hand, people who practice "black" magic are supposed to get their powers from demonic spirits. This puts a person in witchcraft in a very awkward position, because witches say they do not worship the devil. They deny his very existence. They say that the devil is a biblical character, and they do not believe in the Bible. So, a person in witchcraft has to say one of two things: either they are into "white" magic, which is elemental spirits, or they are into "black" magic, which is demonic spirits. Whether it is "black" magic, "white" magic, or whether it is called elemental spirits or demonic spirits, they get their power from the same source. So, if they say they do not believe in demons and yet they say the "black" magician gets his power from demonic spirits, then they are lying.

A prominent leader in the Satanic church says that witches, whether they are into "white" or "black" magic, receive their power from the same source, and that is the devil. To the devil, it doesn't matter what you call the spirits, as long as you call **upon** them.

The devil has a way of changing terms so that people will accept him. It used to be called the occult; now it is the New Age movement. It used to be called demon possession; now it is channelling. A devil called by any other name is still a devil.

Chapter Four

Witches Actively Proselytize Children

"Beware of false prophets, which come to you in sheep's clothing, but inwardly they are ravening wolves." **(Matt. 7:15)**

"Beloved, believe not every spirit, but try the spirits whether they are of God: because many false prophets are gone out into the world." **(1 John 4:1)**

Witches say that they do not proselytize. (*Proselytize* means to change someone's religious beliefs.) Are they being truthful? Here is a quote from an article in a Sunday newspaper. What do you think?

"How would you feel if you had to hide your Star of David or your cross under your shirt? Imagine your outrage if your children were taunted because of your religious beliefs. Or the indignity you would feel at seeing yourself and fellow believers constantly portrayed in the media as green-faced, wart-encrusted crones. And then, to add insult to injury, the city that has long been a mecca for people of your beliefs decides to exclude your kind from planning the commemoration of an event that you believe signifies the height of discrimination against your people. Massachusetts witches are fed up and they aren't going to take it anymore. The Witches League for Public Awareness is intent, once and for all, on bringing witchcraft out of the broom closet and into the public eye." [1]

Let's look at a few cases where witchcraft is being "let out of the closet."

CASE 1

"In October of 1985, Plymouth, Michigan, became embroiled in a major flap over the scheduled appearance of Marion Kucio, also known as the Witch Gundella, at a local high school. The school librarian had arranged Gundella's visit as part of a regular speaker's series. Despite heated protests from Christian parents, the school board was advised by

legal counsel that it would be unconstitutional to cancel the witch's lecture. You see, she was not going to 'attempt to indoctrinate the students in the virtues of witchcraft,' the school lawyer argued. He found on the basis of other presentations she had made that there was 'insufficient basis for interfering with the students' right to receive the information she will impart.'"2

My question is, have our parents and young people been misinformed?

CASE 2

The kids at a public elementary school in Portland, Oregon, were not allowed to celebrate a traditional Christmas this last year. School authorities decided that it would be wrong because religion is not permissible in the classroom. Church and state must be kept separate. Right?

Since Christmas is a Christian holiday, school officials decided that the very word "Christmas" must be forbidden to be spoken. In the place of the annual Christmas event, the school kids would be required instead to participate in the winter solstice program.

On December 19, 1991, the winter solstice was celebrated in the school's auditorium; the theme—"To Celebrate the Return of Light." The cover of the official printed program handed out to students and their parents was revealing. It depicted the sun god (Lucifer, god of light—as a matter of fact, "Lucifer" means "light bearer") and the moon goddess (Diana). Inside the printed program is found this description of the winter solstice program:

"Each child will partake of the sun and moon cake before entering the auditorium, where they will seat

*themselves according to their astrological signs. . . .
Chanting will begin on entering the auditorium. . . .
The sun god and moon goddess will enter with atten-
dants."*

In one segment of the school's solstice program, kids came
in with bar codes stamped on their foreheads. The bar code of
some was read and accepted; other children, who did not have
the proper mark, were rejected. Only those who had the chosen mark were deemed "good and worthy."[3]

To understand what you have just read, you must understand the sacred days of witchcraft. Witches have eight festivals throughout the year:

Major festivals
1. Halloween—October 31
2. Candlemas—February 2
3. Beltane—April 30
4. Lammas—July 31

Minor festivals
5. Yule—December 22—winter solstice
6. Vernal Equinox—March 21—spring equinox
7. St. John's Eve—June 22—summer solstice
8. Michaelmas—September 21—autumn equinox

In the beginning of that article, it was said that we must
keep religion out of schools, yet now we see the winter solstice of witchcraft being used in the place of a Christian holiday. This is what Paddy Slade, a professing witch, in her book,
The Encyclopedia of White Magic, says about the winter solstice:

*"The winter solstice falls right at the end of the
sign Sagittarius, the Archer. This sign rules the ninth
house of the zodiac, which governs philosophy, religion, higher knowledge, and travel."*[4]

It is interesting that while they insist that religion be kept out of school, they use the astrological sign Sagittarius, which supposedly governs philosophy and religion.

The children celebrated the return of light. We read in 2 Corinthians 11:14–15, *"And no marvel; for Satan himself is transformed into an angel of light. Therefore it is no great thing if his ministers also be transformed as the ministers of righteousness; whose end shall be according to their works."*

Eating the cakes was symbolic to heathen worshippers. People who worshipped Baal and Diana would eat cakes before going into worship. In *Witches* by Erica Jong, she states:

> *"This is a ritual by which the high priestess, or leader, of a witch coven takes the power of the goddess into herself, becoming, in effect, the goddess for the duration of the ritual. The witch invokes the goddess within herself—that is, becomes the goddess incarnate."*

That is almost like communion in Christendom.[5] When they take these cakes, they actually take in the goddess and become the goddess in the flesh.

In Jeremiah 44:17–19 not only do you see how the worship of the goddess turned the hearts of the people away from God, you also see how the worship of the goddess turned the woman's heart against her husband. *"But we will certainly do whatsoever thing goeth forth out of our own mouth, to burn incense unto the queen of heaven, and to pour out drink offerings unto her, as we have done, we, and our fathers, our kings, and our princes, in the cities of Judah, and in the streets of Jerusalem: for then had we plenty of victuals, and were well, and saw no evil. But since we left off to burn incense to the queen of heaven, and to pour out drink offerings unto her, we have wanted all things, and have been consumed by the sword and by the famine. And when we burned incense to the queen of heaven, and poured out drink offerings unto her, did we make her cakes to worship her, and pour out drink offerings unto her, without our men?"* You have to understand that the feminist movement and goddess worship go hand in hand. The goddess in reality is the divine mother of the feminist movement.

In another book by the same name, *Witches*, T.C. Lethbridge, an archaeologist from Cambridge University, said this about goddess worship:

> *"The great deity who made the universe and ordered the lives of men was female. She was Diana who, to the Greek world, was known as Artemis. Diana was at first invisible, but she created light in the form of a male consort, Lucifer. He was represented by the sun, the greatest light known to men. Diana, as queen of heaven and darkness was represented by the greatest object in the night sky, the moon."*[6]

The wisest man in the world fell to goddess worship. Did you know that? Satan used the women that Solomon had to turn his heart away from God. First Kings 11:5–6 says, *"For Solomon went after Ashtoreth the goddess of the Zidonians, and after Milcom the abomination of the Ammonites. And Solomon did evil in the sight of the LORD, and went not fully after the LORD, as did David his father."*

Upon entering the auditorium the children were to sit according to their astrological signs. Astrology plays a major part in the worship of witchcraft. This is the frightening part, because according to a Gallup poll:

1. Thirty-two million Americans believe in astrology. That means about one in five adult Americans.
2. There are three times as many astrologers as there are clergymen in the Roman Catholic Church.
3. Over ten thousand people work full-time in astrology

and two hundred thousand work at it part-time.
4. Three out of four newspapers carry horoscopes.

The only reason a person would believe in astrology would be for a religious reason—especially if the person claimed to be an educator. Keep in mind that this was a school program. But let's look at astrology.

Problems Which Stem From Astrology

It is not scientific. How can a person who is a professor say he believes astrology when he knows it is not scientific? The belief which astrology is based on is that the sun circles the earth. Any scientist will tell you the earth circles the sun.

The positions of the constellations have shifted, so the zodiac houses have been shuffled. So in essence, you might say those who totally trust in the zodiac for guidance do not have all the lights on in their house.

People who hold to the accuracy of astrology as gospel would not have a problem with aborting babies, even in the ninth month. Astrology teaches that the life cycle of a person starts at the time of birth, not conception.

> *"The key to astrology is one's natal chart, the map of the heavens at the exact time and place of birth. Based on the horoscope, the celestial patterns are interpreted at any given time concerning events or proposed actions in one's life. Modern astrologers also say the horoscope can be used to discover past lives, karmic lessons to be learned in the present, and hidden talents and skills. It is used in counseling as a means of discovering the self and one's potential."*[7]

Astrology is not able to answer the problem of twins. Why is it that two people can be born within minutes of each other, and yet one can be a doctor and the other a street person; one can be a leader and the other a follower; one can be an extrovert and the other an introvert.

It violates God's Word. Jeremiah 10:2 says, *"Thus saith the LORD, Learn not the way of the heathen, and be not dismayed at the signs of heaven; for the heathen are dismayed at them."* In Isaiah 47:12–13 we read, *"Stand now with thine enchantments, and with the multitude of thy sorceries, wherein thou hast laboured from thy youth; if so be thou shalt be able to profit, if so be thou mayest prevail. Thou art wearied in the multitude of thy counsels. Let now the astrologers, the stargazers, the monthly prognosticators, stand up, and save thee from these things that shall come upon thee."*

What about the bar code on the foreheads of the children? The Bible says in Revelation 14:9–11, *"And the third angel followed them, saying with a loud voice, If any man worship the beast and his image, and receive his mark in his forehead, or in his hand, The same shall drink of the wine of the wrath of God, which is poured out without mixture into the cup of his indignation; and he shall be tormented with fire and brimstone in the presence of the holy angels, and in the presence of the Lamb: And the smoke of their torment ascendeth up for ever and ever: and they have no rest day nor night, who worship the beast and his image, and whosoever receiveth the mark of his name."*

The mark of the beast is also known as the devil's mark. If a witch says they do not believe in a devil, yet encourages young people to take his mark in a school assembly, under the guise of a winter solstice program, maybe now you are starting to understand which witch is which.

CASE 3

Johanna Michaelsen in her book, *Like Lambs To the Slaughter*, states:

"Sixth-graders in Orange County, Florida, practice 'creative writing' by using 'A Witch's Manual,' an eight-page workbook. The children learned, among other things, that 'most witches have a "familiar"— an imp that has taken the form of a cat.' Then they wrote out a list of ingredients that every good witch should keep in her kitchen in order to cast a spell."[8]

The cases are unlimited. The only religion that has been taken out of the public school system is Christianity. Witches say they are into "white" magic, but now you understand that "white" and "black" magic are housed in the same temple.

Chapter Five

Witches and Satanists Have Some Things In Common

"And he built altars for all the host of heaven in the two courts of the house of the LORD. And he caused his children to pass through the fire in the valley of the son of Hinnom: also he observed times, and used enchantments, and used witchcraft, and dealt with a familiar spirit, and with wizards: he wrought much evil in the sight of the LORD, to provoke him to anger."(2 Chron. 33:5–6)

Let's look at some things that Satanists and witches have in common.

Witches use many of the same dates of worship as Satanists do. (Example: winter and summer solstice, and spring and autumn equinox, as well as Halloween.)

Witches try to communicate with the dead, as do Satanists. As a matter of fact, that is the reason Halloween is so important to witches as well as Satanists. In the *Encyclopedia of White Magic*, October 31 is called Samhaine. Samhaine is the end of the witch's year, as well as the beginning.[1]

> *"At Samhaine the veil between our world and the other world is thinnest, and it is thought to be the best time to attract those who have gone before. I must emphasize that, to witches, these are the spirits of the long, lost dead—the old masters and leaders of our race. We are not spiritualists, and do not try to contact Aunt Annie or Uncle Fred to find where they left a will or hid the silver. We understand that there is someone, or something, far greater than ourselves who can help us in our quest for knowledge, light, and truth."[2]*

These statements by professing witch Paddy Slade would be awkward for believers in the craft. Remember, they don't believe in spirits called demons. They only believe in elemental spirits, such as earth, wind, fire, water, and spirit. If they only believe in elemental spirits, then why do they call on human spirits? If the truth be known, witches do believe in spirits other than the elemental spirits of "white" magic. So do Satanists.

Laurie Cabot, Salem's controversial official witch, says,

> *"Like the Puritans, they are still purporting that*

witches are Satanists. We have no devil or Satan in our religion. Witchcraft is a pre-Christian religion. People practiced witchcraft in secret during those times. And we don't know if any of the Salem victims were or were not witches. But by equating witchcraft with Satanism, what they are doing is perpetuating that myth. That is a hate crime."[3]

Some time ago, a prominent leader of the Satanic Church went to Chattanooga, Tennessee, on Halloween to contact Houdini from the grave.

Witches use the same tools of communication with the dead, as do Satanists—such as crystal balls and Ouija boards. If you thought the Ouija board was just a game, think again. According to Johanna Michaelsen,

"The talking board became a national rage during the First and Second World Wars, when people desperately wanted to know the fate of their loved ones in battle. Spiritism has traditionally experienced revivals during times of war and other catastrophes. It also became fashionable among the ladies to employ the board as a parlor game during the early 1900s. That's all the ever-alert IRS needed. In 1920 they declared the board a game, and as such subject to taxation. By 1920, the creator had sold over three million of them! The case went to court. Never mind that Attorney Allen Fisher contended that the Ouija 'is a form of amateur mediumship, and not a game or sport.'"[4]

But the Ouija board was around well before the 1900s. I remember some time ago visiting St. Augustine, Florida, supposedly the oldest city in America. I had the opportunity to visit the oldest toy shop, and as I looked above the door frame, to my surprise, there hung a Ouija board.

Trying to contact the dead is directly contrary to Scripture. Deuteronomy 18:10–11 says, *"There shall not be found among you any one that maketh his son or his daughter to pass through the fire, or that useth divination, or an observer of times, or an enchanter, or a witch, Or a charmer, or a consulter with familiar spirits, or a wizard, or a necromancer."*

NINE ABOMINATIONS IN DEUTERONOMY 18:10–11

Human sacrifice—the use of children to appease these false gods.

Divination—fortune telling.

"Astrology is perhaps the oldest system of divination and prophecy. Astrology is based on the Hermetic belief that the physical world is a reflection of the cosmos ('as above, so below'). In astrology, the positions of the planets, sun, and moon in the zodiac constellations exert influences on the lives of mankind and the world below. A complex art, astrology is used by some modern witches as a divinatory and spiritual development tool."[5]

Observer of times—astrology.

"Your astrological sun sign tells a lot about you— but far from everything there is to know! Renowned astrologer Sybil Leek shows you how to obtain a much more accurate and insightful self-portrait in Moon Signs.*"*[6]

Not only was Sybil Leek a world-renowned astrologer, she was also a world-renowned British witch and occult scholar. She authored four books on astrology, as well as two books on witchcraft.

"According to Leek, Crowley announced to her grandmother that little Sybil would someday pick up where Crowley would leave off in occultism. The last time she saw him was in 1947, shortly before his death."[7]

By the way, Aleister Crowley was called the "Beast" by his mother. He was one of the founding fathers of our modern-day Satanist movement.

Enchanter—a person who uses chants to cast spells.

Witch—a person who says that witches are make-believe does not know the Word. There are severe consequences for being a witch in the Scripture punishable by death. This is mentioned nine times in the Bible. Exodus 22:18 says, *"Thou shalt not suffer a witch to live."*

Charmer—objects that are made by someone to protect you or to curse others.

Consulters with familiar spirits—a familiar spirit is a spirit that impersonates a person who is dead.

A wizard, magician, or sorcerer—often a term for a male witch.

Necromancer—someone who claims to contact the dead (as Whoopie Goldberg did in the movie *Ghost*). One of the biggest blockbuster hits in the last few years was the movie *Ghost*. The advertisement for the movie reads as follows:

"Don't miss the romantic thriller that had everyone believing in the power of love to reach past death! Demi Moore and Patrick Swayze are the perfect couple torn apart by his murder. Their love endures through medium Whoopi Goldberg."[8]

A Gallup poll indicates the following from a poll of five hundred and six teens between the ages of thirteen and seventeen:[9]

WHAT SUPERNATURAL PHENOMENA DO TEENS BELIEVE IN?

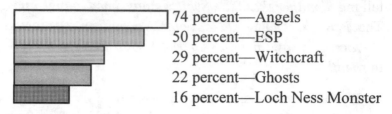

74 percent—Angels
50 percent—ESP
29 percent—Witchcraft
22 percent—Ghosts
16 percent—Loch Ness Monster

Do people who die have a desire to talk to the living? According to Luke 16, a rich man died and had a desire to warn his brothers not to come to this place called hell. Luke 16:28–29 says, *"For I have five brethren; that he may testify unto them, lest they also come into this place of torment. Abraham saith unto him, They have Moses and the prophets; let them hear them."*

Wouldn't someone believe and desire to be saved if they saw someone come back from the grave? Matthew 27:52–53 says, *"And the graves were opened; and many bodies of the saints which slept arose, And came out of the graves after his resurrection, and went into the holy city, and appeared unto many."* Could you imagine your husband coming home for supper after he had been dead for a week? Or a teacher's eyes when she sees a student who has been dead three days walk into her class? Not everyone got saved, even though they did see people come back from the dead.

A person of witchcraft may ask, "Don't you talk to the dead when you talk to Jesus?" My answer to that is found in Luke 24:5–7, *"And as they were afraid, and bowed down their faces to the earth, they said unto them, Why seek ye the living among the dead? He is not here, but is risen: remember how he spake unto you when he was yet in Galilee, Saying, The Son of man must be delivered into the hands of sinful men, and be crucified, and the third day rise again."*

The angels made it clear, Jesus wasn't dead any longer, He was alive. If I tried to talk to Buddha, I would be talking to a dead man. If I tried to talk to Mohammed, I would be talking to a dead man. But Jesus Christ is a living Savior. That is why Christians do not seek the living among the dead.

Going hand in hand with talking to the dead is the belief in reincarnation.

THREE DANGERS INVOLVED IN REINCARNATION

1. People can become possessed during a reincarnation trance. I remember some time ago, I was watching the *Phil Donahue Show,* and a woman was on the program who had never been hypnotized before. This man came on the set and said, "I want you to close your eyes, and count backward—ten, nine, eight. . . ." As he got down to about five or so, suddenly you could see terror in the woman's eyes, and he said, "Don't be afraid. Follow the light, and he will protect you." Who was the light he was talking about? It wasn't the light of the world. It was Lucifer—the light bearer.
2. People commit suicide in hopes of a better life the next time around.
3. Reincarnation gives people a false hope for life after death.

FIVE THINGS THAT PEOPLE USE TO JUSTIFY THEIR ACTIONS THROUGH REINCARNATION

Homosexuals can explain their lifestyle by reincarnation. Reincarnation teaches that a person is a homosexual because in a past life a man may have been a woman, and in this life he still desires men. The Scripture says in Leviticus 20:13, *"If a man also lie with mankind, as he lieth with a woman, both of them have committed an abomination: they* *shall surely be put to death; their blood shall be upon them.* " God never says that homosexuality is right. That is the reason reincarnation and Christianity don't go hand in hand at all. What else does the Bible say about homosexuality?

In Romans 1:27 we read, *"And likewise also the men, leaving the natural use of the woman, burned in their lust one toward another; men with men working that which is unseemly, and receiving in themselves that recompence of their error which was meet.* " People try to tell me that homosexuals are born that way. I don't believe that. I have never known a doctor to walk into the hospital and say, "You are the proud parents of a five pound, four ounce, homosexual!" No, they are not born that way; they are made that way.

They can justify not helping the needy by this karmic law. Karmic law means that you must pay for the wrongs that you committed in your past life. The only problem with this is, you don't know what you did wrong in your past life unless you consult a psychic who also can talk to the dead— which again is an abomination.

One thing a person must understand, there cannot be a law without a law-giver. People who believe in reincarnation do not believe in a personal God. But without a personal God as a law-giver, there can be no law. Example: If there were no laws, you could drive one hundred miles an hour down your street, because there is no law-giver. But because there is a law-giver, there is someone who has made a law saying, "You cannot drive one hundred miles an hour down this road; you must drive no faster than twenty-five miles an hour." There is a law-giver that made that law.

In karmic law they do not believe in a personal God. But if there is no personal God, who makes up the laws? Who says, "You are going to be born in Australia; you are going to be born in Japan. You are doing good; you are doing bad. Ah, you hit him in the mouth—you go back as a wart." Who keeps the laws of what is good and what is wrong?

Reincarnation says all the problems you have are self-inflicted. Rabindranath "Rabi" Maharaj wrote a book entitled *Death of a Guru*. In this book he tells of his aunt who was raising him. His father died when he was seven and his mother was going to college. His aunt was paralyzed from the waist down. While she was at the hospital she found a Bible, brought it back, and started reading it to the children. Her husband, who was a Hindu, became angry when he heard her reading the Bible—the very Word of God—to these children. It made him so angry that he grabbed her and pushed her wheelchair down the stairs. And as she lay bleeding at the bottom of the steps, she thought only, "I must be paying for something I did in my last life."

There are those who say that Christianity is a religion of guilt. Yet reincarnation says you are guilty and doesn't even give you the knowledge of how to take care of your guilt. Romans 4:21–25 says, *"And being fully persuaded that, what he had promised, he was able also to perform. And therefore it was imputed to him for righteousness. Now it was not written for his sake alone, that it was imputed to him; But for us also, to whom it shall be imputed, if we believe on him that raised up Jesus our Lord from the dead; Who was delivered for our offences, and was raised again for our justification."*

As a Christian, we are not filled with guilt, but filled with a hope. The word impute means to charge to someone else's account. This is like getting a blank check signed by the richest man in the world. To those of us who are saved, our sins have been charged to another account, and that account belongs to our Lord and Savior Jesus Christ.

It can justify murder. Some people in the New Age movement believe that Hitler did the Jews a favor by killing them because, apparently, they had a bad karma.

It can justify being unfaithful to your marriage part-

ner. Reincarnation teaches that people have what are called soulmates. They are people who die and somehow get together in other lives. This is a great rationale for those who want out of a marriage. They can simply say that they married the wrong soulmate. Does this happen? I remember talking to a man named Steve. Steve was in the New Age movement, and his wife was a channeller. He went on a quest to try to find spiritual enlightenment, but when he returned he was really enlightened to find out that the spirit inside his wife had told her that she had made a mistake in marrying him. The spirit said that he was not her true soulmate. Now, that would be hard to swallow, wouldn't it?

1. Witches and Satanists both use spells and incantations as a part of their religion.
2. Witches as well as Satanists believe in divination or fortune telling.

In Acts 16:16–19 we read, *"And it came to pass, as we went to prayer, a certain damsel possessed with a spirit of divination* [you see, divination is not a gift; it is a spirit] *met us, which brought her masters much gain by soothsaying: The same followed Paul and us, and cried, saying, These men are the servants of the most high God, which shew unto us the way of salvation. And this did she many days. But Paul, being grieved, turned and said to the spirit* [notice Paul never talked to the woman; he talked to the spirit—she was probably a channeller], *I command thee in the name of Jesus Christ to come out of her. And he came out the same hour. And when her masters saw that the hope of their gains was gone, they caught Paul and Silas, and drew them into the marketplace unto the rulers."*

Many people believe that fortune tellers are just fraudulent people. They believe these people are just very clever con artists. This is not true. Some are possessed by a spirit that can manipulate the future. You must understand that after the spirit left the woman, she was no good at foretelling the future.

Chapter Six

Witches and Satanists Use the Media to Recruit

"Professing themselves to be wise, they became fools."
(Rom. 1:22)

Witches and Satanists use the media to recruit. This is an entry in the *The U.S. Chaplain's Manual* from the Church of Satan on ethics, recruiting, and relationships. They were questioned concerning how the Church of Satan recruits new members. They responded with the following:

> *"The church does not proselytize but welcomes inquiries from honest potential Satanists who hear about the church from the various books about it, the mass media, or word-of-mouth."*[1]

This is also from the *U.S. Chaplain's Manual*. This entry is from the American Council of Witches, and they were asked the same question. It was answered thusly:

> *"Witches do not proselytize, but welcome inquiries from those who hear about the craft by either word-of-mouth or the media."*[2]

For two totally different organizations and two totally different entries, they surely have some definite similarities. If two totally separate and different people wrote these two documents, without one another's knowledge, they must have been led by the same spirit. So, in essence, they say they do not proselytize, but they both have one thing in common. They both have their religion propagated by the media.

THREE WAYS THAT THE MEDIA HELPS WITCHCRAFT

By giving a distorted view of witchcraft. They make a witch look like a wicked, ugly old hag, so that when an attractive woman claims witchcraft as her religion, people become more curious and let their guard down.

They introduce good witches to combat the bad, ugly witches. This gives an image that some witches can be trusted as allies for good. You notice that good magic always wins over bad magic. This leads a person to believe that it is okay to practice witchcraft, if it is for good. If I were to ask you, "Are all witches bad?"—what would you say?

You may think back to *Bewitched* and Samantha—she wasn't a bad witch, was she? Then you might think of Sabrina, the teenage witch from the *Archie* comic books. But probably one of the strongest images may have come from *The Wizard of Oz*. Anyone who saw the beautiful witch of the north would not have one thing bad to say about her.

Just to prove my point, let's talk about *The Wizard of Oz*. Is this family classic just a family classic, or could it be classic witchcraft?

First, you notice that all the witches in the movie are actually directional. For example, the house landed on the *wicked witch of the east*. Dorothy was hounded by the *wicked witch of the west*. Then she was helped by the *good witch of the north*. Logic would have us believe that if the wicked witches were from the east and west, then the good witches would be from the north and south. Yet, you are never introduced to the "good witch" from the south. Not once in the movie does the "good witch" from the south appear. Why?

The answer may lie near the end of the movie. Do you remember how the good witch of the north helped Dorothy get home? Dorothy was discouraged because she found that the Wizard of Oz was really a fake, and all hope of her returning home was gone. Then the witch of the north told Dorothy that she had the power latent inside her to go home all the time. According to satanic teaching, it says, *"Say unto thine own heart, 'I am mine own redeemer.'"* Would we dare think that sweet, little Dorothy may have learned that everyone has a latent power to perform good magic? Could she have subtly been the fourth witch? The "good witch" of the south? Do you remember the first question that was asked of Dorothy by the good witch of the north? *"Are you a good witch, or are you a bad witch?"* Dorothy said, *"I'm not a witch at all. Witches are ugly."* The Munchkins laughed, and Glynda, the good witch of the north, said, *"Oh, no, only evil witches are ugly. I am a good witch."* See, she was beautiful. Do you know what that image evokes? It gives a false security that if a witch is attractive, he or she can be trusted as good and not evil. Could she, Dorothy, have subtly been the fourth witch? You know where her house came from— the south. Keep in mind that good witches are from the south and were beautiful. I would say that Judy Garland, or Dorothy, was very attractive. Was she possibly the *witch of the south*?

Witches do believe in directional spirits which we will talk about a little later in the section on The Magic Circle.

Remember in the beginning of the movie, Dorothy runs away from home to save Toto, and finds herself seeking spiritual guidance from a professor and a crystal ball. He looked into the crystal point. A very important point is that Dorothy sought occult guidance before she ever went on her journey to Oz. Now we know the professor was a fake at that point, but he said that this crystal ball came from Isis and was used by the Egyptians. Again, Isis was a goddess worshipped in Egypt. How convenient it was that Dorothy would just so happen to stumble upon a person who claimed to have the spirit of divination.

Dorothy finds herself seeking occult guidance throughout the whole movie. Who could ever think one bad thought about the sweet, innocent girl who would sing, "Somewhere Over the Rainbow," before the rainbow was used as a symbol for the New Age movement? By the way, for some of you who do not know what the rainbow means in the New Age movement, it means basically the arch or bridge that leads from the natural to the supernatural. Without a doubt, Dorothy crossed the bridge in *The Wizard of Oz*. The sad thing about it is that Judy Garland, who played Dorothy, died of suicide. Miss Garland may have found the rainbow, but she never found the light of the world.

Let me prove my point of how the media promotes witchcraft. Right now some of you are angry that I would bring up *The Wizard of Oz* while talking about real witchcraft. Some of you are thinking that I am, excuse the expression, "witch hunting." Right now, some of you would like to debate me on all the good wholesomeness of this movie. All I can say is that witches are right—the media can be their best source of recruitment. The media has craftily changed your biblical perspective of witchcraft. Not one time is witchcraft mentioned in a good context in the Bible. Philosophically you might say that witches are not all bad. But biblically they are always bad. As a matter of fact, in Exodus 22:18, the Bible says that *"Thou shalt not suffer a witch to live."*

SYMBOLISM BEHIND THE WIZARD OF OZ

1. They followed the yellow brick road. Yellow is often used as a color to refer to gold. There is only one place I have ever heard about golden streets—that is Heaven. (Remember, her house did spiral northward.)

2. This golden road led Dorothy and her friends to the Emerald City, where the all-powerful and all-knowing wizard lived. Omnipotence and omniscience are two attributes that belong only to God. They found that the all-powerful and all-knowing wizard was a fake. He was just a man that people had elevated to become a supreme being. In a world filled with agnostics who are confused about the existence of God, could this be a reference to God? See, God is all-knowing, all-powerful, and yet many would have us to believe God does not exist; that He is

just an elevated person that we created to be a supreme being.

3. The final thing to consider is the pure dose of humanism as the end result. After finding out that the wizard was a man, they found out that they had all the power inside themselves. The Tin Man really did have a heart; the Cowardly Lion really was not a coward; the Scarecrow had the ability to think the whole time; and Dorothy had the ability within herself to go home any time.

Humanism teaches that there is no God, and that we all have the power within ourselves to succeed. There may be those who say I am making too much out of *The Wizard of Oz*. Witches are just make-believe. Before you make that statement, maybe you might want to read about how witches are gearing up to change your mind:

*"But in Wiccan circles, Cabot is considered a high priestess of the religion and a leader. In 1986, she and other witches formed the Witches League for Public Awareness, a non-profit, tax-deductible organization dedicated to correcting misinformation about their religion. They publish a newsletter and pamphlets, like law memorandum that outlines the 1985 U.S. District Court decision that ruled **witchcraft is a legitimate religion**. The most recent newsletter discusses an Air Force ruling that approved religious holidays for witches and a U.S. District Court case in which a federal judge ruled against the Salvation Army because it fired a woman who practiced witchcraft."*[3]

To illustrate how witchcraft is viewed from God's perspective, not media perspective, we must look at Nineveh. You remember Nineveh. It was the city Jonah went to. It was the city that God cared so much about that he sent Jonah, special third-day delivery, via whale. This city was so big, it took three days to walk around it. The walls were one hundred feet high and broad enough to drive a chariot on. It had more than twelve hundred towers that people could adorn. Yet, it was a wicked city. Jonah 3:4 says, *"And Jonah began to enter into the city a day's journey, and he cried, and said, Yet forty days, and Nineveh shall be overthrown."* These words convicted the whole city and they all repented.

Then one hundred and fifty years after one of the greatest revivals in history, God sent another prophet whose name was Nahum, to Nineveh. Even though Nahum means "the comforter," his message was anything but comforting. It was a message of doom. Yet the people would not repent. Why? The answer is found in Nahum 3:4: *"Because of the multitude of the whoredoms of the well-favoured harlot, the mistress of witchcrafts, that selleth nations through her whoredoms, and families through her witchcrafts."* This verse tells us that witchcraft destroys nations as well as homes.

THREE DANGEROUS SIMILARITIES BETWEEN NINEVEH THEN AND OUR WORLD NOW

Witchcraft became not only accepted, but well-favored. My nephew, some time ago, was cutting out some pictures in his class. The teacher then handed out some pictures of witches and told the students to cut out these witches. My nephew looked at his teacher and said, "I can't cut out pictures of witches; I don't believe in witches." The teacher told him he didn't understand—these were good witches. Talk about lacking in discernment.

There are many Christian people who would be ready to defend *The Wizard of Oz*. If it were just an entertaining movie and not an indoctrinating movie, why are Christians so mad when I suggest it to be bad? It all depends on what you use as your plumb line. If you use the Bible, you will probably have no trouble with making the right decision. But if you use philosophical ideas, you will be headed in the wrong direction.

The Bible says it sells nations—that means it is marketable. Today, everything on the market has something to do with witchcraft. Witchcraft today is a very marketable commodity. In fact, it is so bad that I have a lot of parents say to me, "Everything I've got for my children is bad, bad, bad. What can my children play with?" Understand that before the Antichrist sets up his kingdom, he's going to have to set up an Antichrist society. Everything you hear today is dealing with magic—it's like magic, it works like magic, magic this, magic that. Witchcraft is very marketable.

Finally, the Bible says that Nineveh's families were sold into witchcraft. Did you know that witchcraft is family oriented? That's right, witchcraft today is rated "G." Top family movies, like *Witch Mountain, Escape to Witch Mountain*, and *Return to Witch Mountain*, by Disney are all family oriented.

The Care Bear Movie had a witch in it, as did *The Little Mermaid*. (Again, don't say they were bad witches unless you believe there are such things as good witches.) These are just a few of the hundreds of "G" rated movies that do not have vulgarity and nudity, but are loaded with witchcraft. Did you know that the Billy Graham film, *The Prodigal*, was rated PG by the Motion Picture Industry of America? Do you know why? Because the Motion Picture Industry said that children should not be exposed to Christianity without the consent of their parents. Yet, witchcraft today is all rated "G," but is it family oriented? Please understand, Satan has a family-oriented program. He wants desperately to reach your family. Those involved in witchcraft are also referred to those who study the craft. Strangely enough, *craft* is the root word for "crafty." And one would have to admit that they live up to their name.

The third way the media encourages witchcraft and Satanism is they give a distorted view of Christianity. Let's look again at some quotes from the *U.S. Chaplain's Manual*. What is witchcraft's role in relationship with other religions? According to the American Council of Witches,

> ". . . cooperation with other religions are cordial, except those groups which have sought to persecute and defame the Craft."[4]

Can anyone guess what religion they are talking about? The answer is Christianity. To my knowledge, Christianity is the only religion that has ever come out against witchcraft. This is a quotation from the *U.S. Chaplain's Manual*, submitted by the Church of Satan. Their relationship with other religions is as follows:

> "The Church of Satan stands as a gathering point for all those who believe in what the Christian Church opposes."[5]

In essence, witchcraft and Satanism stand with open arms, and gathers all those who oppose Christianity. Here's a test to see if our society holds to the Christian belief or the satanic or witchcraft belief, via the media:

- Does the Bible teach homosexuality is wrong? Yes.
  Does the Church of Satan teach homosexuality is wrong? No
  Does the Church of Wicca teach homosexuality is wrong? No.
- Does the Bible teach that adultery and fornication are wrong? Yes.
  Does the Church of Satan teach that adultery and

fornication are wrong? No.
Does the Church of Wicca teach that adultery and
fornication are wrong? No.

● Does the Bible teach that we have only one true
God, Jehovah? Yes.
Does the Church of Satan teach there is one true
God, Jehovah? No, they make themselves god.
Does the Church of Wicca believe in the one true
God, Jehovah? No, they have many gods.
Does the media believe in the one true God, Jeho-
vah? No, they adhere to the god of humanism.

● Does the Bible teach that occult powers are bad?
Yes.
Does the Church of Satan teach that occult powers
are bad? No.
Does the Church of Wicca teach that occult pow-
ers are bad? No.

So you see, practicing Satanism and witchcraft is not putting on a black robe, praying to the devil, or burning candles
at midnight. It is a value system that is totally contrary to
Christianity. You must understand that everything that we
believe as Christians is opposed by Satan.

How does the media encourage anti-Christian views?
When was the last time you saw a movie that made a Christian look sensible? The movie *Footloose* made the villain of
the town a preacher who was against teenagers dancing.

The movie *Cape Fear* (1991) made the psychopathic killer
a born-again Christian. In one scene of the movie, the villain
tells a young lady he doesn't hate her father; he prays for her
father. Then he proceeds to molest her.

The NBC made-for-TV movie which aired on Monday,
September 7, 1992, was titled *In the Best Interest of the Children*. It portrayed the mother of the children as being men-

tally ill. When they were coming to get her to put her in a mental institution, she huddled up with her children asking Jesus to help her. They all cried and again she looked at the children and told them to get down on their knees and pray to Jesus. Then she looked at her little daughter and called her a Judas and told her that she had betrayed her! The daughter told the mother that she had not betrayed her. She had not said anything at all.

Again we see the Christian portrayed in a negative fashion. She was mentally ill. You know that is not the first time Christians have been called mentally ill. That is the image that the media is putting out toward Christianity today.

Again we see the Christian portrayed in a negative fashion in the movie about Jim Jones and the Guyana tragedy. This movie portrayed Jim Jones as a fundamentalist preacher gone crazy. Jim Jones was never a fundamentalist preacher. He was a socialist New Ager. But you have to understand this was a perfect opportunity to put Christianity in a negative context.

How about David Koresh? Hollywood could not even wait until the end of the stand-off before they went into production on the made-for-television movie. From the very beginning, this group was referred to as the Davidian cult. The key word here is "cult." There is an extreme hatred in our country for cults. People in America are more tolerant of drug dealers than they are of cults. I must admit, I, too, have a low tolerance level for extremist cults. The thing is, where does the government or the media get off calling a religious group a cult? A cult is a religion that does not hold to the basic doctrines of the Christian faith. Neither the government nor the media adhere to the Christian faith. So why do they have the right to call any religion a cult?

Will the government and the media one day declare their religion of humanism to be the true religion? Will they one day declare that any other religion is a cult? Will this give them the right to kill people? Will people of the future accept this kind of barbarianism? The answer is YES!

Revelation 13:4–7 says, *"And they worshipped the dragon which gave power unto the beast: and they worshipped the beast, saying, Who is like unto the beast? who is able to make war with him? And there was given unto him a mouth speaking great things and blasphemies; and power was given unto him to continue forty and two months. And he opened his mouth in blasphemy against God, to blaspheme his name, and his tabernacle, and them that dwell in heaven. And it was given unto him to make war with the saints, and to overcome them: and power was given him over all kindreds, and tongues, and nations."*

If we say the Bible teaches us to kill witches, we would be cruel, non-tolerating bigots. Yet, during the Tribulation it will be totally accepted to kill saints. It is amazing how many Americans believe the government was right to kill some innocent women and children because the media called them cultists.

These are just a few blatant misrepresentations of Christianity. When was the last time you heard a news report putting the Christian Church in a good light? Not lately. Yet who has not heard about Jim Bakker and Jimmy Swaggert? Since those scandals have been exposed, people look at Christians a little bit differently. When I tell people that I am an evangelist, the first thought is not that I am a Christian serving God, but that I am a charlatan and a dishonest person. This was not the view ten years ago. Ten years ago, if you told someone you were an evangelist, they would call you "Reverend." Now they grab their wives, hide their children, and hold their back pocket!

How has this affected Christianity? It has made people hostile toward Christianity. Women who have prayed for years for their husbands to go to church, now find themselves hearing the words, "I told you all those people at church were hypocrites." And their husbands are going to die and go to hell, because the media has given a misrepresentation of Christianity. Yes, there is a Jim Bakker, and yes, there is a Jimmy Swaggert, but if the media would spend as much time showing all of the Christians who have served God and all that we have done over the last thousands of years for communities, the Jimmy Swaggerts and Jim Bakkers would just be a drop in the bucket!

You used to be able to talk to people about the Lord and even if they did not agree with it, they would still hear you out. Today, the tolerance level toward Christianity is near zero. You might say the worse Christianity looks, the better witchcraft and Satanism look. So the next time you see Christians being laughed at and made fun of, understand that it is a planned deception to turn the hearts away from God, which automatically turns their hearts toward Satan.

Chapter Seven

Satan Is "Trolling" for Souls

"In meekness instructing those that oppose themselves; if God peradventure will give them repentance to the acknowledging of the truth; And that they may recover themselves out of the snare of the devil, who are taken captive by him at his will." **(2 Tim. 2:25–26)**

According to the *Dictionary of Satanism*, the definition of *troll* is, *"In Teutonic religion, an earth demon or a personified non-human power."*[1] The Bible tells us to beware of the snares of the devil. A snare is a trap. As a boy, I grew up near the Gulf of Mexico. It was not uncommon to see men and women selling fresh shrimp and fish on the side of the road. When I was very young, I wondered how they caught them. Trolling for shrimp is not uncommon in Louisiana. Trolling is where boats let down their nets and pull them through the water. Fish and shrimp, unaware of the nets, soon find themselves entangled in the web without any way to escape.

A very common doll that is being distributed today is called a *troll*. Parents buy these little creatures with a Don King hairstyle and think, "Isn't it neat that trolls are once again becoming popular among children?"

Maybe you ought to know a few things about these ugly little dolls, made cute. According to the book, *Man, Myth, and Magic*, trolls may be a little different than you picture them.

First of all, they are elemental spirits. For those of you who have forgotten, elemental spirits are what witches use for magic. Northern European mythology belongs to the supernatural fairy community, which was once assumed to exercise dominion over nature. Again, "white" witches use nature in magic. This was a class of spirits regarded with considerable apprehension, since all elementals were known to be capricious, treacherous, and frequently hostile.[2]

Secondly, in Norway and Sweden they were dull-witted, huge-nosed, hairy cannibals. The noses were used to smell out their human prey.

"They were also good workers. They were builders by trade. But their wages were usually the souls

of men. Giant trolls were frequently credited with building mighty structures like castles, bridges, and churches, and legends abound describing how they were cheated of their wages (usually human souls) by their sharper-witted clients."[3]

The third thing that really alarms me is that girls are the only people who ask me about trolls. You may ask, why is this so alarming? According to the description of trolls in *Man, Myth, and Magic,*

> *"A rapid degradation in the status of the trolls followed the advance of Christianity into Northern Europe which had the effect of transforming all Teutonic elementals into what can only be described as Christianized devils. Many of the basic characteristics of the troll are clearly discernible in the attributes of devils. The troll wife-stealers became in time, the demon lovers. The incubus seduce women in their sleep."*[4]

In the occult, they teach that there are two sexual demons. One is the succubus spirit that materializes as a woman to have sex with men. The other is the incubus spirit, which is the spirit that is supposed to materialize as a man in order to have sex with a woman. Are these toy makers ignorant of the material I just gave you? Then why are they primarily marketing trolls to little girls? What makes me so angry is that these toy companies are deliberately making this product for little girls. This puts a parent in a very uncomfortable position. How do you explain what is wrong with these trolls to a little six-year-old girl?

Here is an actual letter we received:

Mr. Benoit:
 I attended your meeting in Tennessee. I just had

to write to thank you. I came home after one of the meetings and decided to rid our home of trolls and turtles. My little girl, who is only four years old, loves the trolls.

But I have to tell you the story behind my little girl. She was a "perfect" baby in that she slept most of the time as an infant. She was a very content girl. She slept all night from four weeks of age until the day of July 14, 1992 when she turned three years of age. For her third birthday she received a troll that was almost as tall as she. She changed over night. She stopped sleeping through the night, her attitude changed, her whole disposition changed.

I assumed the "terrible twos" had set in at three and shrugged it off. The Monday night of your meeting we took all the trolls and turtles from the house. She has slept all night since. Even her disposition is changing back to that sweet loving little girl. I just had to write to you. I want to say thank you a million times over.

Melina

Recently, I spoke to a group of teenagers in a Bible study on the subject of trolls. A girl came up after the service feeling very bad about the purchase she had made of a troll for her four-year-old niece. She asked me, "How can I tell my niece what is wrong with the gift I just gave her?" That's a hard question. My best answer would be, "God does not like trolls. They are of the devil."

Does the Scripture suggest that demonic spirits can have sex with women or men? Let's look at Genesis 6:1–5, *"And it came to pass, when men began to multiply on the face of the earth, and daughters were born unto them, That the sons of God saw the daughters of men that they were fair; and they took them wives of all which they chose. And the LORD said, My spirit shall not always strive with man, for that he also is flesh: yet his days shall be an hundred and twenty years. There were giants in the earth in those days; and also after that, when the sons of God came in unto the daughters of men, and they bare children to them, the same became mighty men which were of old, men of renown. And God saw that the wickedness of man was great in the earth, and that every imagination of the thoughts of his heart was only evil continually."*

There are two theological interpretations of these verses. The first is that godly men were having sexual relationships with ungodly women. The one problem with this interpretation is that godly men and women, even today, marry unsaved people. Their offspring are never physical mutations. The offspring of these relationships were giants.

The second interpretation is that the sons of God were fallen angels that took the form of men to have sex with women. Those were incubi. One problem with this theory is that angels are created and humans are born. Can fallen angels produce offspring in women? These are both debatable theories.

Here is my point: If theory number one is right, then your daughter's troll is just a toy; but, if theory number two is right, your daughter could be open for demonic attack.

I was doing a television program some time ago, and the subject of trolls was being discussed. The pastor who was interviewing me asked if we could take a break. He had tears in his eyes as he told me a story of his daughter winning some trolls at an amusement park. She brought them home and immediately began crying out in the middle of the night. They did not understand what was wrong. When I talked with this paster later, he told me they had rid their house of the trolls, and that their daughter was not crying out at night any more.

Some time ago I was asked to talk to a thirteen-year-old girl in a Christian school in Alabama who was infatuated with the rock group Duran Duran. Duran Duran got their name from the movie *Barbarella*, starring Jane Fonda. It was a movie about a man who could have sex with a woman during an out-of-body experience. To my surprise, I had read in a teen magazine an article about Duran Duran. The group said they have received letters from young girls who claimed to have had sex with members of the rock group in the same fashion as had happened in that movie. This article was still fresh in my mind when I was called to talk to this girl. I would like to reiterate that this girl was in a Christian school. This girl was observed by others kissing a picture of the group she carried with her constantly, as well as actually talking to them. So when I sat in the principal's office with this girl, I asked her if she knew where Duran Duran got their name. Without hesitation she told me about the movie. Yes, she had watched it. So, I asked her point-blank if she had ever had sex with Duran Duran. Before she ran out of the office, she said, "That is none of your business!"

This girl did not look at me and ask if I were crazy for asking such a ridiculous question. No, this girl had some kind of an experience with Duran Duran. She personally is a believer of incubus, whether we believe it or not.

The final problem I have with trolls is that now some of them have a magic stone in their stomachs. I will talk about this later with the Care Bears. *"If you believe strongly enough, all of your wishes will come true."* That is what the commercial says about trolls. Crystals are used in witchcraft as well as in the New Age movement. In witchcraft and Satanism, this is called a charm. My point is, if a child begs you for a troll, when the only purpose of that troll is to grant wishes, that child is now a believer in magic stones. Congratulations, your child now makes believe the same thing a witch really believes. The Church of Satan says that the best way to get a person into the occult is through fantasy. Fantasy says you can wish on a stone, and it will happen.

Chapter Eight

Lucifer Is Quite a Charmer

"There shall not be found among you any one that maketh his son or his daughter to pass through the fire, or that useth divination, or an observer of times, or an enchanter, or a witch, Or a <u>CHARMER</u>, or a consulter with familiar spirits, or a wizard, or a necromancer. For all that do these things are an abomination unto the Lord: and because of these abominations the Lord thy God doth drive them out from before thee." **(Deut. 18:10–12)**

A charm is an object or thing that a person aligns himself with in order to gain good luck. It is not uncommon for even good Christian people to wish me good luck. I realize that many times it is just out of habit or lack of a better phrase to wish one well. I would much rather have someone say, "May the Lord bless you." Words such as luck, charm, and amulets are generally associated with witchcraft or superstition.

Superstition often becomes a way that Satan uses to control peoples' lives. I remember when I was a boy, we were barely allowed to go outside of our home on Friday the 13th for fear of receiving some kind of bodily harm. Was I childish to believe that anything associated with the number thirteen was bad luck? Do you realize that many high-rise apartments, hotels, and office buildings do not have a thirteenth floor? Do you know why? Many people will not sleep on the thirteenth floor of a hotel. Some would believe that working on the thirteenth floor of an office building would hold an evil fate for the company. Is the number thirteen an unlucky number? Then why do people fear it?

Would you feel eerie if you had to cross the path of a black cat? Would you ever think about walking under a ladder? Would you enter a state of depression if you broke a mirror, even though you knew you would not have seven years of bad luck?

I am amazed at how well-educated people react to superstition. Probably the most superstitious people in the world are involved in sports. If a professional baseball coach thought Christians were bringing the team bad luck, he would trade them in a heartbeat. I personally know of such a case where that really happened. Some baseball managers would never step on the baseline because that is bad luck. One professional baseball team several years ago was in a batting slump. They brought in a person to try to remove the curse from the bats.

Probably the most famous curse in baseball is associated with Babe Ruth. It is said that a curse was put on Boston for trading the "Babe" to New York. Do you realize that Boston has not won a World Series since they traded him? Witches have been consulted to try to remove the curse, but it hangs on. In 1986, Boston was only one out away from winning the World Series when a ground ball was hit between the legs of the first baseman. It was the error that cost them the winning run. To this day, people still believe in the curse of the "Bambino." It's funny—I was watching television just this weekend after writing this chapter, and I saw them letting loose balloons, and they had brought in a man to remove the curse of the Bambino because Boston isn't doing very well this year either!

Some pitchers would never think of going to the mound without their lucky shirt or lucky hat. Some even have a rabbit's foot. You know what I've never understood about a rabbit's foot, that foot didn't do too much for the rabbit that owned it at first!

Some wear what is called the good luck charm, some wear the Italian horn around their neck for prosperity. The Italian horn is a little, wiggly kind of horn. Is this just foolishness, or is it bondage?

I remember one time a girl came up to me after one of my services. This young lady was having problems with demonic activity in her life. While I was talking to her, I noticed that she had an Italian horn around her neck. I asked her if she knew that that particular charm was of the devil? She replied, "I know that." Then she started to tell me a bizarre story of how many nights the devil would come to her in a dream. He would tell her that he owned her soul because she wore his charm. Then she proceeded to tell me that all through my message, the horn on her neck continued to burn her chest. She said sometimes it was so bad, she had to lift it from off of her neck to keep it from burning her. I said, "Listen, do you want to be set free from all of that?" She said that she did. Do you know how she got that charm? Strangely enough, at her graduation from a Christian school, a boy gave her the charm and told her that as long as she wore it around her neck, she would always know that somebody loves her.

You should always become suspicious of a person who gives you a charm and tells you to never take it off. She took that thing and even though she did not know it was a cursed thing, Satan visited her in her dreams and she had demonic activity in her life. She still didn't want to take it off. It became bondage to this girl. So that night we had that amulet taken off of her neck, and we burned it. We prayed that the girl be set free. Deuteronomy 18:11–12 explicitly tells us not to adhere to a charmer or a maker of charms, *"Or a charmer, or a consulter with familiar spirits, or a wizard, or a necromancer. For all that do these things are an abomination unto the* LORD: *and because of these abominations the* LORD *thy God doth drive them out from before thee."* You see, charms are not always superstitious; sometimes it can be supernatural. Lucifer is not into blessings; he is into bondage.

Chapter Nine

Witches Do "Knot" Play Fair

*"And the spirit of Egypt shall fail in the midst thereof; and I will destroy the counsel thereof: and they shall seek to the idols, and to the charmers, and to them that have familiar spirits, and to the wizards. And the Egyptians will I give over into the hand of a cruel lord; and a fierce king shall rule over them, saith the Lord, the L*ORD* of hosts." (Isa. 19:3–4)*

When I say witches do not play fair, I spell it "k-n-o-t." Here is an excerpt from a letter we received:

Dear Mr. Benoit:

I am a campus police officer for a small community college. I have been studying the occult and satanic crime for some time now, and when I came upon one of your brochures I was intrigued.

I have recently heard of a form of satanic ritual that involves ropes and knots. However, I have not been able to come up with any other information on it. If you know of any other things that I might be interested in, please send it my way.

Jeff

Let me explain. In the *Encyclopedia of Witches and Witchcraft*, the definition of *knot magic* is,

"The tying and untying of knots is used to bend and release energy in many folk-magic spells and formulas. The ancient Egyptians and Greeks tied knots in cords for love spells. The 'Knot of Isis,' a red jasper amulet wound in the shroud of royal Egyptian mummies, summoned the protection of Isis and her son Horus for the dead in the next world.'"[1]

Several years ago, a pastor friend of mine called me asking questions about a strange thing that had happened to him. He knew a young couple who had experienced paranormal activity in their home. When he was asked to visit them, he reluctantly went. After spending a little time with the couple, he was convinced that demonic activity was going on their home. The pastor asked them if they had anything in the home that was linked with demonism, such as Ouija boards or tarot cards. The couple said that there was nothing like that in the home to their knowledge. The pastor asked if he might be able to visit the attic. To his surprise, he found ropes hanging all over the attic with knots tied in them. After more investigation he found that the previous tenants were a motorcycle gang that practiced "black" magic. Apparently, these ropes were supposed to have an attraction for demonic spirits. The best I could figure out was that some demons are territorial, and the ropes acted as a boundary for these evil spirits.

I have a special reason for telling this story. I was alarmed as I read a story by Johanna Michaelsen in her book, *Like Lambs To the Slaughter*.

For several years now, a kindergarten teacher in California has provided ghosts for her pupils to commune with at Halloween. One mother told of how her little boy was sent home with a note from the teacher informing the parents that their child would be bringing home a "special friend" the next day. The child was to nurture his "friend," name it, and talk to it as a part of a special class project that was designed to "develop the child's imagination." The next day the boy came home with a sealed envelope and instructions that his parents were not to touch it; only the child was allowed to open the envelope. Mom said, "You bet!" and promptly opened it. Inside was six inches of orange wool string with a knot tied a quarter of the way up to make a loop resembling a head. The mimeographed "letter" that accompanied it read as follows:

Haunted House
001 Cemetery Lane
Spookville

Dear Customer:
Thank you for your order. Your ghost is exactly what you ordered. You will find that your ghost is attached to an orange string. Do not untie the special knot until you are ready to let your ghost go.
Your ghost will tell you when it is hungry and what it

prefers to eat. It will sleep in the air beside you all day. It especially likes quiet places where there are cobwebs, creaky boards, and corners.

If you follow the above directions, you will have a very happy ghost.

Yours truly,
Head Ghost

The mother, a Christian lady, didn't cotton to the idea of her son taking in a pet ghost, however housebroken. She was also a little suspicious of her six-year-old being addressed as "Dear Customer." So she confiscated the thing and put it in the garage on a shelf until she could decide what to do with it. The next day her sister was in the garage on an errand, unaware of the matter of the "ghost-on-a-rope." Suddenly she was frightened by the sense of a threatening presence around her. She heard the sound of a cat hissing in the corner and something like a "chatting doll" mumbling incoherently at her. Later that night, they threw the "ghost string" into the garbage pail, prayed to bind and remove the entity, and were never bothered by the "presence" again. This family had no trouble whatsoever believing that a spirit had indeed been sent home with their little boy, and that it didn't much like having been assigned to a Christian household.[2]

The Bible tells us to not be ignorant of Satan's devices, lest he deceive us. I am sure that you are now starting to understand the true deceptiveness of Satan.

Chapter Ten

Smurfs Are Not "True Blue"

"But there was a certain man, called Simon, which beforetime in the same city used sorcery, and bewitched the people of Samaria, giving out that himself was some great one: To whom they all gave heed, from the least to the greatest, saying, This man is the great power of God. And to him they had regard, because that of long time he had bewitched them with sorceries. But when they believed Philip preaching the things concerning the kingdom of God, and the name of Jesus Christ, they were baptized, both men and women." (Acts 8:9–12)

At first glance, the Smurfs seem harmless. They work together, play together, and seem to be one big, happy family. Yet a closer look will show their true colors.

Gargamiel is the villain in the story line. He has two uncontrollable passions. First, he loves evil magic, and second, he hates good, little Smurfs. Gargamiel has been seen casting spells in the name of Beelzebub, which means "lord of the flies," or "prince of demons." Beelzebub is mentioned in Mark 3:22-30: *"And the scribes which came down from Jerusalem said, He hath Beelzebub, and by the prince of the devils casteth he out devils. And he called them unto him, and said unto them in parables, How can Satan cast out Satan? And if a kingdom be divided against itself, that kingdom cannot stand. And if a house be divided against itself, that house cannot stand. And if Satan rise up against himself, and be divided, he cannot stand, but hath an end. No man can enter into a strong man's house, and spoil his goods, except he will first bind the strong man; and then he will spoil his house. Verily I say unto you, All sins shall be forgiven unto the sons of men, and blasphemies wherewith soever they shall blaspheme: But he that shall blaspheme against the Holy Ghost hath never forgiveness, but is in danger of eternal damnation: Because they said, He hath an unclean spirit."*

The name Beelzebub, strangely enough, was used in association with blaspheming against the Holy Spirit. When the scribes and Pharisees used the name Beelzebub in response to the work of the Holy Spirit, Jesus warned them that they were walking dangerously close to the unpardonable sin. Should this name Beelzebub be used in a cartoon? Believe me, blasphemy is not cartoon material!

Gargamiel has also used the magic circle in order to cast spells. The magic circle is also called the ceremonial circle, protection circle, sacred circle, and unbroken circle in demonism.

"In witchcraft, the magic circle provides a sacred and purified space in which all rites, magical work, and ceremonies are conducted. It offers a boundary for a reservoir of concentrated power and acts as a doorway to the world of the gods. The circle symbolizes wholeness, perfection, and unity; the creation of the cosmos; the womb of Mother Earth; and the cycle of the seasons; and birth-death-regeneration. Within the circle it becomes possible to transcend the physical, to open the mind to deeper and higher levels of consciousness."[1]

"The witch works within a magic circle and uses four primary magical tools, which correspond to the elements:

> *the athame (or sword)—fire*
> *the pentacle—earth*
> *the chalice—water*
> *the wand—air."*[2]

Gerald B. Gardner, the English witch credited with reviving modern interest in witchcraft, has eight ways to make magic, usually used in combination, which are:

1. **Meditation or concentration**
2. **Chants, spells, invocations**—Chants are chanted or sung slowly at first, then increased in tempo to shrieks.
3. **Trance or astral projection**—In astral projection, one leaves the body behind and travels in the astral realms in the astral body, or double, a spirit replica of the physical body.
4. **Incense, wine, and drugs**
5. **Dancing**—Witches join hands and dance around the magic circle, speeding up the tempo until the

power is at a peak. When the magic is released, they drop to the floor or ground.

6. **Blood control and use of cords**—Binding parts of the body with cords restricts blood flow and alters consciousness, which facilitates the opening of the third eye for clairvoyance, and astral projection.

7. **Scourging**—Religious mystics have used flagellation for centuries. In witchcraft, it ideally is light, slow, and steady. Scourging is a milder form of blood control, for it draws blood away from the brain.

8. **The Great Rite**—Ritual sexual intercourse between the high priest and high priestess of the coven is said to release tremendous magical power.[3]

Those involved with "black" magic have the pentagram or the five-pointed star inside the circle. Two points are at the top, two points on the side, one point downward. This is supposed to make the head of a goat. The two top points represent the horns of the goat. The two side points represent the ears and the downward point is the chin of the goat.

In "white" magic, the two points are downward representing the two legs of the man. The two points on the side are the extended arms of the man, and the one pointed up is the head of the man.

The points of this circle are supposed to have significance also. The east point represents Lucifer. We read in Isaiah 14:12–16, *"How art thou fallen from heaven, O Lucifer, son of the morning! how art thou cut down to the ground, which didst weaken the nations! For thou hast said in thine heart, I will ascend into heaven, I will exalt my throne above the stars of God: I will sit also upon the mount of the congregation, in the sides of the north: I will ascend above the heights of the clouds; I will be like the most High. Yet thou shalt be brought down to hell, to the sides of the pit. They that see thee shall narrowly look upon thee, and consider thee, saying, Is this the man that made the earth to tremble, that did shake kingdoms."*

The north point represents the elements or Belial earth. The name Belial means vileness or ruthlessness. This is a better description of the trolls. In 2 Corinthians 6:14–18 we read, *"Be ye not unequally yoked together with unbelievers: for what fellowship hath righteousness with unrighteousness? and what communion hath light with darkness? And what concord hath Christ with Belial? or what part hath he that believeth with an infidel? And what agreement hath the temple of God with idols? for ye are the temple of the living God; as God hath said, I will dwell in them, and walk in them; and I will be their God, and they shall be my people. Wherefore come out from among them, and be ye separate, saith the Lord, and touch not the unclean thing; and I will receive you, And will be a Father unto you, and ye shall be my sons and daughters, saith the Lord Almighty."*

The west point represents water or Leviathan. Leviathan means "one who dwells in the sea of humanity"—like the god Dagon who is half-man, half-fish. Isaiah 27:1 says, *"In that day the LORD with his sore and great and strong sword shall punish leviathan the piercing serpent, even leviathan that crooked serpent; and he shall slay the dragon that is in the sea."* Interestingly enough, *The Little Mermaid*, the counterpart to Dagon, was told not to investigate humanity.

What does the Bible say about bringing into the home images that resemble gods? Deuteronomy 7:25–26 says, *"The graven images of their gods shall ye burn with fire: thou shalt not desire the silver or gold that is on them, nor take it unto thee, lest thou be snared therein: for it is an abomination to the LORD thy God. Neither shalt thou bring an abomination into thine house, lest thou be a cursed thing like it: but thou*

*shalt utterly detest it, and thou shalt utterly abhor it; for it is
a cursed thing."*

So what does the Bible say about bringing a cursed thing
or an image of a god into your home? I mentioned Dagon a
few minutes ago. Dagon, if you will remember the story, was
the god that they put next to the Ark of the Covenant. It kept
falling on its face. Archaeological digs show that the god
Dagon was half-man and half-fish. Now, it is really interesting that on *The Little Mermaid* they introduce a new character that is half-man and half-fish—a "Mer-man." Not only
that, but Titan, the father, is half-fish and half-man. So you
know what is going to happen: a lot of people are going to
buy these characters of Titan and "Mer-man," and they will
be bringing replicas of the Old Testament god Dagon into
their home.

Other references to Leviathan are found in Job 41:1–2,
14–34.

The south point represents fire, or Satan. Satan means
"the adversary or opposing spirit." The name of Satan is used
fifty-two times in the Bible. In Zechariah 3:1-4 we read, *"And
he shewed me Joshua the high priest standing before the angel of the LORD, and Satan standing at his right hand to resist
him. And the LORD said unto Satan, The LORD rebuke thee, O
Satan; even the LORD that hath chosen Jerusalem rebuke thee:
is not this a brand plucked out of the fire? Now Joshua was
clothed with filthy garments, and stood before the angel. And
he answered and spake unto those that stood before him, saying, Take away the filthy garments from him. And unto him
he said, Behold, I have caused thine iniquity to pass from
thee, and I will clothe thee with change of raiment."*

Yes, Satan is the accuser of the brethren, and you know,
he is right. We are unworthy of God's mercy and grace. Yet
though our sins be as scarlet, we are made white as snow. We
have the righteousness of Christ imputed to us.

I remember speaking one night in a small town in the state of Washington. After the service, a young man approached me. He was trembling as he told me that he had just talked to a demon-possessed person. Because many people misinterpret mental illness, hyperactivity, and other psychological disorders as demon possession, I asked him why he thought that. He replied that as they were standing on the porch of the church, all of a sudden his friend said, "Listen and you'll hear the dogs bark." Immediately, the dogs started to yelp. Then his friend said, "Go tell Dave Benoit I'm going to kill him."

I was not anxious to meet a person who wanted to kill me. As I began to drink another glass of punch, another person approached me and said that Rick wanted to see me. I knew who Rick was. I had had lunch with him earlier that day. When I walked into the room with him, I asked him what he wanted. He replied, "What do you think about a person who wants to kill somebody?" I said, "You mean, like you kill me?" He said yes.

I quickly responded, "You can't even touch me unless God gives you permission." Do you realize that the Bible tells us that angels encamp about them that love God? The devil cannot touch you unless God first gives him permission. Besides, if a Christian is killed by a Satanist, that Christian would just be ushered into the presence of Jesus. I like what one evangelist said when a man threatened to kill him: "Don't threaten me with eternal life."

I do not believe that demons can harm you if you are in a right relationship with Jesus Christ. I do believe that demons can harm you if you openly and willfully invite them into your home or life through occult tools.

I asked the young man this question: "Do you want to be set free?" He responded, "Yes, I do." I was trying to identify the demon inside the boy. I asked the demon to identify himself. The boy responded, "Rick." I said, "I'm not talking to you Rick; I'm talking to you, devil. What is your name?" The spirit said, "My name is Lucifer." I told him that he was a liar, because the devil would never put himself into a position to be cast out.

All of a sudden, Rick's head fell down and a gruff voice came from within him: "Azarel." And for the next forty-five minutes we dealt with a demon by the name of Azarel. That name may not mean anything to you. At the time, it meant nothing to me. After another meeting in another church, a man who had been involved in demonism told me the meaning of the name Azarel. When people in demonism want to commit suicide, they call on Azarel, who was Lucifer's personal death angel. I was also surprised when I found out that Azarel is also the name of the cat on the Smurfs. What is Azarel's primary objective on the cartoon? It is to catch and kill little Smurfs.

Unless you were well versed in demonism you would not have chosen that name. The names for these characters are not made up; they come from demonism.

Chapter Eleven

Something Smells a "Little Fishy" With *The Little Mermaid*

"Dagon—The national god of the Philistines, whose most famous temples were at Gaza and Ashdod. Its form had the face and hands of a man, and the tail of a fish." (Young's Analytical Concordance, p. 218)

"Then the lords of the Philistines gathered them together for to offer a great sacrifice unto Dagon their god, and to rejoice: for they said, Our god hath delivered Samson our enemy into our hand." (Judg. 16:23)

"When the Philistines took the ark of God, they brought it into the house of Dagon, and set it by Dagon. And when they of Ashdod arose early on the morrow, behold, Dagon was fallen upon his face to the earth before the ark of the LORD. And they took Dagon, and set him in his place again." (1 Sam. 5:2–3)

Some time ago I was speaking at a church in Virginia. The pastor thought the material that I was presenting on witchcraft and rock music was just a little too frightening for little children. So, while I was in the main auditorium speaking against witchcraft, the pastor's wife was showing Disney's movie, *The Little Mermaid*, to all of the young children.

The next day I saw the video cover lying next to the VCR. I asked him why his wife was showing a movie depicting a mermaid who made a pact with a witch. His response was, "But, David, she was a bad witch." The problem with this is, if you are going to tell your children there are bad witches, then you are just reinforcing the idea that there are good witches. For a moment, I was confused as to how I should respond to him. Then the Lord revealed something to me. In these movies where witchcraft is portrayed as evil, good people make a pact with the evil witch, and then escape through their own craftiness. If I was the devil, I would want every little child to believe that they can make a pact with a witch and then be able to walk away from it.

You will never see Hollywood portray Jesus Christ as the only way out of witchcraft. We as believers know that Christ is the only true way out of witchcraft. The reason I am telling this story is not to belittle this pastor and his wife; they are godly people. It is to show you how crafty and subtle Satan is even in infiltrating the strongest Christian homes.

It is dangerous to make a pact with the devil. One night I was speaking in a church and a girl approached me during the invitation. She was trembling uncontrollably as she told me that she had got into trouble and made a pact with the devil. If he would get her out of trouble, she would give him her soul. She reached down and her hands began to shake. She grabbed the bottom of her skirt—a long dress all the way to her shoes—and lifted it above her calf. When she got it above her calf, I could see a demonic image tattooed in her leg. Her hands were shaking as she said, "I made a pact with the devil, and I can't get it off. He's got my soul, Mr. Benoit, he's got my soul!" That's not a joke!

Now you can see why I do not take lightly when *The Little Mermaid* tells our children that it is all right to make a pact with a witch. People put this in their mind and then when they really make a pact with the devil, they find out that the devil does not play fair. I looked at that girl and said, "Young lady, the devil doesn't have your soul if you are willing to give it to Jesus Christ. God doesn't look at your leg; He looks at your heart."

And by the way, you can't make a pact with the devil to give him your soul. For you see, before a person is saved, the devil already has your soul. You don't barter with something that someone already has. I told the young lady that God could set her free from what she had gotten into. What I am really worried about is that a lot of young children watching *The Little Mermaid* today may find a real witch to make a pact with tomorrow. They are going to believe that they can walk out of witchcraft as easily as they walked in.

Did you know that the mer-people were supposed to dwell in an underwater world of great splendor? Mermaids lured their victims, and they were kept prisoners in the "Kingdom Beneath the Waves."[1]

Several dangerous teachings come from *The Little Mermaid*, including:

1. It is all right to make a pact with a witch.
2. The Little Mermaid disobeyed her father in studying humans (that is rebellion, which we know is the sin of witchcraft). And did you know that when the Little Mermaid disobeyed her father continuously, she was as much into witchcraft as Ursella the witch was?

3. It teaches that there is another way to escape witch-craft without the power of Jesus Christ.
4. That mermaids are good.

Did you know there is a mermaid working in Africa? They worship a goddess of the sea. Her name is Mammy Water Spirit. Oddly enough, she is half-woman and half-fish.

In Revelation 17:5 we read, *"And upon her forehead was a name written, MYSTERY, BABYLON THE GREAT, THE MOTHER OF HARLOTS AND ABOMINATIONS OF THE EARTH."* As we look at the popularity of goddess worship today, would it be unfair to have Dagon now appear as a female named Mermaid?

Did you know that Ariel is mentioned in the Bible, as well as in witchcraft material? Ariel in witchcraft would fall under the elemental spirit earth according to *The Complete Book of Witchcraft*.[2] In the Bible it is another name for Jerusa-lem (see Isaiah 29). The name means "lion of God." Apparently, Ariel is associated with the judgments.

Turtles Are "Zeroes," Not "Heroes"

LEGS CROSSED, THUMB & TWO FINGERS TOGETHER...,
REMEMBER.... JUST LIKE THE TURTLES DO IT.

"For the weapons of our warfare are not carnal, but mighty through God to the pulling down of strong holds." (2 Cor. 10:4)

An interesting study was made some time ago about how people perceive reptiles. Here is how the study was conducted. A rubber snake was placed on a road, then those doing the study hid themselves in a bush to see how motorists would respond. Almost without fail, the motorists who saw the snake ran over it. Yet when the snake was replaced with a fake turtle, almost every motorist swerved to miss it. Apparently, the motorists felt that the snake was a threat, while the turtle was cute and would harm no one.

Maybe that is the mindset we have toward the Teenage Mutant Ninja Turtles. They are funny, cute, and non-threatening. This isn't how I perceive them. This from *USA Today*:

> "*Teenage Mutant Ninja Turtles II: The Secret of the Ooze* . . . *encourages violent and anti-social behavior among kids, says a college professor who surveyed seventy-three teachers in nineteen states. The findings: Kids emulate the karate chopping and pizza chomping* . . . *says study co-author Diane Levin, associate professor of education at Wheelock College. 'The way the Ninja Turtles work out their difficulties is by socking each other and knocking each other,' said survey respondent Hanne Sonquist.*"[1]

America is really hurting when she can find no better role models for our children than four street people in a half shell. I remember one Fourth of July, I bought a large quantity of bottle rockets. I was lighting them and letting them go in the sewage drain. Smoke gushed out and I jokingly told my children that I was getting the Teenage Mutant Ninja Turtles. They laughed uncontrollably, because my children do not believe in the Turtles. Do these turtles exist? This article was found in the *USA Today* newspaper:

> "*The Turtles Play the Palace: The sewer-smell-*

ing Teenage Mutant Ninja Turtles inadvertently are prompting kids in Great Britain to go underground, literally. Several children, imitating their reptilian heroes, have been rescued recently from sewers and culverts, prompting authorities to warn parents."[2]

These children do not know the difference between fantasy and reality.

DANGERS OF THESE REPTILIAN HEROES

They are into the religion of Zen Buddhism. Splinter is the Turtles' Zen master. Zen is quickly becoming the religion of Hollywood. Actors such as Patrick Duffy and Patrick Swayze are into Zen Buddhism. Even Stephen Nichols, formerly of *Days of Our Lives*, played Zen therapist Schyler Gates on NBC's *Santa Barbara.* According to *USA Today*,

"The actor, who has studied Eastern philosophy for twenty years, says, 'It is serendipitous that this role should fall into my lap.'"[3]

According to the book, *The Three Pillars of Zen*, the three pillars are teaching, practicing, and enlightenment. In the editor's preface, we find these words:

"Zen is a religion with a unique method of body-mind training, whose aim is satori, that is self-realization."[4]

If you are not aware of Eastern religious teaching, *satori* or self-realization means that you realize that you are god. Shirley MacLain has already realized that she is god. She takes off all her clothes on a mountain top and says that she is god! I can see Gabriel talking to God and saying, "There's not much competition these days, is there?"

John Denver says that one day he will be so complete, he will not be a man, but he will be god. Even Charlotte, North Carolina, has its own Zen Meditation Society. They teach that the Buddha nature is in everyone. Anne Bancroft, in her book *Zen*, gives the purpose of Zen:

> *"The aim of Zen training is to attain the state of consciousness which occurs when the individual's ego is completely emptied of itself and becomes identified with the infinite reality of all things."*[5]

Basically what Bancroft was trying to explain is that like in *Star Wars* when Luke Skywalker was flying through the maze with Darth Vader hot on his trail, he was unconsciously connecting with the infinite reality of all things. Luke heard an audible voice from his master telling him to let go and let the force take control.

Were these teachings accidentally interjected into the *Star Wars Trilogy?* Not according to Irvin Kershner, director of *The Empire Strikes Back.* He said that he wanted to introduce some Zen here because he did not want the kids to walk away just feeling that everything is shoot-em-up, but that there's also a little something to think about in terms of yourself and your surroundings. Billy Dee Williams landed the part in the *Star Wars Trilogy* because of his belief in Zen Buddhism.

Yoda became the mouthpiece in the *Star Wars Trilogy* for Zen Buddhism. He was basically the Zen master. Yoda was to *Star Wars* what Splinter is to the Teenage Mutant Ninja Turtles.

In the book *Zen*, we find this statement:

> *"All martial arts are life and death struggles with one's own ego. They can be used for self defense, but their real aim is self knowledge, leading to self-realization."*[6]

Could the Turtles be leading our children into the hands of Eastern religion via martial arts classes? The Turtles explain that in their book *Teenage Mutant Ninja Turtles—The Storybook Based on the Movie.*

> *"The next few days found the Teenage Mutant Ninja Turtles training with purposeful energy. From dawn till dusk they worked out. They trained with blindfolds on, learning to use senses they had not known they possessed."*[7]

The plot of the movie was that the Turtles had lost their Zen master, Splinter, who had been captured by a wicked villain named Shredder. The Turtles had no idea where to find him. So one day, one of the Turtles, Leonardo, was practicing the art of Zen meditation on a tree stump while closing his eyes, doing controlled breathing, and putting his fingers together to keep the cosmic energy inside his body, which is an occult and New Age practice. All of a sudden, the movie shows Splinter in captivity. He lifts his head and calls to Leonardo. How did Splinter know that Leonardo was trying to contact him? We are not talking about martial arts here; we are not talking about self-defense. We are talking about an occult teaching called telepathy. He ran back and told the other Turtles that Splinter was alive! They asked, Who? He told them that he knew Splinter was alive because he had communicated with him.

> *"That night Leonardo and his three rather skeptical brothers sat around a campfire in the woods. 'Now just do what I told you,' Leonardo explained. 'Everybody close their eyes and concentrate. Hard.' His brothers reluctantly obeyed. There was silence, broken by the crackling of the fire and the shrill throb of the tree frogs. Just when the others were beginning*

*to get a little itchy, an image of Splinter—transparent
and ghostly—appeared wavering above the flames.
'I am proud of you, my sons.' The Turtles gasped.
'Tonight you have learned the final and greatest truth
of the ninja—that ultimate mastery comes not of the
body . . . but of the mind. . . . Together there is nothing
your four minds cannot accomplish. Help each other.
And always remember the force that binds you, the
same as which brought me here tonight. The true force
which I gladly return with my final words: I love you,
my sons.'"*[8]

There are a few observations that I have made from reading this material. First, to communicate with Splinter it had
to be done with telepathy. Secondly, their meeting was around
a bonfire (or balefire, which is a ritual bonfire in witchcraft).
Conveniently enough, it was observed during a full moon.
This too is common in witchcraft worship. The third thing I
noticed is that he appeared out of the fire, which is one of the
elemental spirits used in witchcraft. The fourth thing, he said
the truth behind the ninja was not of the body, but of the
mind. The whole teaching behind the occult is mind over
matter. Finally, he says that it was "the force" that brought
him there and would keep them together. It is interesting they
keep using the word *force*. They used it in *Star Wars*, and
they also used it in *Teenage Mutant Ninja Turtles*. It is interesting that the force he was talking about was fire. As we
talked earlier—fire represents Satan.

Daniel 11:37–38 gives a description of the Antichrist as
follows: *"Neither shall he regard the God of his fathers, nor
the desire of women, nor regard any god: for he shall mag-
nify himself above all. But in his estate shall he honour the
God of forces: and a god whom his fathers knew not shall he
honour with gold, and silver, and with precious stones, and*

pleasant things."

One of the dangerous things about the Teenage Mutant Ninja Turtles is when they do teach their meditation, they do it with the force. There are also New Age teachers who guide children through this. They say, "How many of you have seen the *Teenage Mutant Ninja Turtles?*" And all of these little children raise their hands. "How would you like to put your fingers together like Leonardo did?" And they put their fingers together. "Remember, Leonardo used to breathe and think real hard. Can we think real hard?" All these children are so anxious to do it, because they saw it on *Teenage Mutant Ninja Turtles.* Then the teacher says, "Maybe if you think hard enough, maybe you can meet a friend like Splinter; maybe you can meet a spirit-guide, like Splinter." These children are listening to these New Age teachers. And do you know what is happening? Some of them are being led into meditation and actual demon-possession, because they are looking for a spirit-guide.

I believe that even happens to Christian children. Do you know why? Because these little children say, "I know the Teenage Mutant Ninja Turtles can't be bad because my mom and I watched the movie together. We all laughed at parts. Surely, if there was something wrong, my mom wouldn't buy me Turtles. And I know my grandma; she loves Jesus and she goes to church all of the time. She watched the movie and didn't see anything wrong with Leonardo putting his fingers together, so maybe I will put my fingers together."

The Teenage Mutant Ninja Turtles become a reinforcement for New Age teachers who lead their children in meditative classes. And your child may be a target, too.

Before the word *force* was used in *Star Wars* and *Teenage Mutant Ninja Turtles—The Movie,* it was a description of the god the Antichrist would worship. Before you claim this as an impossibility, maybe you might consider a book entitled *Meditating with Children* by Deborah Rosman. Deborah has a degree in psychology and is an educational consultant to many school districts. The *East-West Journal* reviewed this book, and gave this recommendation:

> *"Among the most enlightening of the new teaching books . . . a well-illustrated tool of practical psychology . . . the absence of a religious point of view in the book makes this volume an excellent learning vehicle."*[9]

Does this book lack religious content? Think again! Consider this quote:

> *"Discuss astronomy, the solar system, the sun, and the planets, and then relate to the twelve signs of the zodiac with simple astrology. Have each child write down his name and sun sign on a separate slip of paper. Have the children of the same sign sit next to each other, then the same elements—fire, earth, water, and air—sit together."*[10]

Page 60 recommends fire meditation; page 64 recommends earth meditation; page 66 recommends water meditation; page 68 recommends air meditation; and page 138 describes the evolution of the soul.

Samuel Silverstein tells how he accidentally stumbled onto meditation with his third grade class.

> *"By accident, I happened on this method of having the children rest their heads on their desks, close their eyes, breathe deeply, and then concentrate on something. Later, when I studied the methods used by the mystics of the Far East, I realized that this method was somewhat similar to the ones used in their searches into the secrets of life. The mystics led lives*

*of solitude in caves, used special deep-breathing ex-
ercises to adjust their inner bodies for attunement,
and meditated on what they were searching for. When
the children closed their eyes, they were in solitude;
when they breathed deeply, they were using one of
the breathing practices of the mystics; and when they
concentrated on something, this was the same as meditation.* "[11]

Strangely enough, Silverstein and the Turtles seem to have
the same agenda. This is a conversation between April and
Splinter, a quote from a *Teenage Mutant Ninja Turtles Special Comic Book*:

"**Yoga** *is an exercise, an art, a science, and a way
of life for many people. It was discovered by the ancient Hindus three thousand years ago. You have probably noticed that the initial pain when you crossed
your legs is gone. And you've become accustomed to
being in what yogis call the* **lotus** *position. Remember, with* **yoga** *you must calm both your mind and
body.* "[12]

Another thing Silverstein just happened to stumble onto
was the psychic abilities in children.

"*If we had ESP, or psychic abilities, as most children probably have, we could look inside our physical bodies and see what is going on in our spiritual
bodies.* "[13]

The mystery is—did John Gentile of Archie Comics read
Child Spirit when he wrote "Doomsday Hassle at Banshee
Castle"? "*In the name of Bonnie Prince Charlie, you have
the second sight, Lassie! ESP—Extra Sensory Perception, the
psychic gift of the highlander.* "[14]

HERE ARE A FEW QUESTIONS

1. Was violence one of the sins of Noah's day? Yes. Genesis 6:11, 13 says, *"The earth also was corrupt before God, and the earth was filled with violence. . . . And God said unto Noah, The end of all flesh is come before me; for the earth is filled with violence through them; and, behold, I will destroy them with the earth."*

2. Could these Turtles be setting up children for New Age teachers?

3. Could the Teenage Mutant Ninja Turtles be a subtle reinforcement for evolution? Are they teaching that mutants can turn out good?

Chapter Thirteen

Bart Simpson Has His Own Values System

"There is a way which seemeth right unto a man, but the end thereof are the ways of death." (Prov. 14:12)

"For the LORD knoweth the way of the righteous: but the way of the ungodly shall perish." (Ps. 1:6)

Simon's values clarification is a popular teaching tool to reinforce situation ethics. In essence, the Bible calls it *"every man did that which was right in his own eyes."* This encourages young people "that if it feels good, do it." This is pretty much the philosophy of Bart Simpson. This cartoon, produced by the Fox Network, totally undermines the true values of the Judeo-Christian ethic belief. Is this a harmless cartoon? I don't think so.

Personally, I have never seen a complete program of the Simpsons. Yet I have seen enough clips and commercials to tell me there is something seriously wrong with the program.

He never calls his father "father"; he calls him "Homer." In one November episode of "The Simpsons," Bart is asked to give thanks for their Thanksgiving dinner. Bart then lifts his eyes toward heaven and tells God that they worked for the money for this food, thanks for nothing. Of course, his father, the stooge, corrects him for being irreverent. Other names for his father are stupid and idiot.

Do children pick up on this imagery? Sometime ago, I was at a service station filling our car with gas. A lady was dragging her son by the arm because he wanted a soda to drink. Now this child was probably about pre-school age. Yet, his terms for his mother were "You idiot, you stupid, you idiot." He repeated this all the way to the car.

What does this type of behavior produce? Could it lead to child abuse? Take a parent who is frustrated, overworked, or has had too much to drink. Would they tolerate for even a second a child who refers to them as stupid or an idiot?

For years, we have listened to Dr. Spock's advice that tells us not to spank our children. Many parents have complied with the advice. Now we find that child abuse is on the rise. Could it be that a parent instead of disciplining their children lovingly, explodes in uncontrollable anger because the problem gets out of hand?

The Simpsons are not the only family with a very poor outlook on the male image. It seems today that bashing the male figure and adoring the female figure is in vogue. Could this be by design or by accident? Psychologists tell us that we get our concept of God from our fathers. Obviously, when a person hears God speaking to Moses or to Noah, it is always a male voice.

When Jesus taught his disciples to pray, He said, *"Our Father which art in heaven"* (Matt. 6:9), not our mother. As a matter of fact, when you look into satanic literature, Lucifer is depicted as having a goat's head and a woman's chest. Quite a contrast from Jesus who was called the Lamb of God.

Fertility deities have always been a vital part of pagan worship. So, when I see the male figure distorted in situation comedies, I don't always see it as a laughing matter. Here are just two examples of recent sitcoms that reinforce this argument.

1. *The Cosby Show*—Have you ever noticed how Bill Cosby, who plays the father on this program, is always the fall guy for every mistake? We are not talking about an idiot. This man is a medical doctor, yet he blunders most of what he does. If there is a debate between Claire, his wife, and himself, she is always right. And he is always wrong.

2. *Family Matters*—The father again is treated like a stooge. Every time he tries to fix something, he totally wrecks the place.

A person must admit, with child abuse and the poor example of fathers it is very easy to lose a true concept of God.

Chapter Fourteen

"He's Man" and "She's God"

"And when the townclerk had appeased the people, he said, Ye men of Ephesus, what man is there that knoweth not how that the city of the Ephesians is a worshipper of the great goddess Diana, and of the image which fell down from Jupiter? Seeing then that these things cannot be spoken against, ye ought to be quiet, and to do nothing rashly." (Acts 19:35–36)

Some time ago, as I was speaking in a church, I just happened to mention the program *He-Man, Masters of the Universe.* A lady approached me after the program with her nine-year-old son. She was angry about the comments I had made about He-Man.

She said, "My son has the entire 'Masters of the Universe' set, and he's not a devil worshipper." I said, "Ma'am, I never said that your son was a devil worshipper; I simply said that Jesus was the Master of the universe, not He-Man."

So, I casually looked down at the little boy and asked him about the green substance that comes out of Castle Grayskull. The boy replied, "Oh, you mean ectoplasm?" Now, that's a pretty big word for a little boy, wouldn't you say? His mother looked at me and said, "Ecta-what?" I replied, "Ectoplasm. Don't you know what ectoplasm is?"

For all of you who do not know what ectoplasm is, let me explain. Sometimes when a psychic tries to make contact with the spirit world, they will have convulsions and spittle will sometimes flow from their mouth, and demons will materialize on the spittle. The puddle that is left is ectoplasm. Basically, it is the remains of a demon. By the way, if you bought a *Ghost Busters* set for Christmas, they gave you a free can of ectoplasm to put in your child's room. Just one quick note about *Ghost Busters*. I do not think ghosts are spirits of those who died, they are demonic spirits. And it is very dangerous when you teach your children ghosts can be busted by a *Ghost Busters* gun. It is very dangerous to teach our children to take lightly demonic activity.

What do He-Man and She-Ra teach our children? They teach that He-Man is the master of the universe. Is that true? No. Jesus Christ is the Master of the universe, not He-Man. I'm afraid that we are presenting too many images of God to our children.

They are told He-Man is the master or god of the universe. They are told that there is a real Santa Claus. The problem with parents who reinforce make-believe is that children do not know when you are telling them the truth.

Gene Roddenberry, the creator of *Star Trek* and *Star Trek: The Next Generation*, died a seventy-year-old humanist. A humanist is a glorified atheist. When Roddenberry was interviewed by the *Humanist Magazine*, he said that he didn't believe in Jesus. Roddenberry says,

> *"At five and a half years old, I learned there was no such thing as a Santa Claus. I must admit, there was sorrow when I think of reasons why he could not have existed. But, I think the same thing when I think of Jesus and the church."*[1]

By the way, Roddenberry's mother was a devout Baptist when Roddenberry found out his mother had lied to him. It is very dangerous when we teach our children there is a real Santa Claus. I know that people get angry when I point out that when they tell their children that Santa Claus gave them the gifts, they are actually taking glory away from God.

He-Man gets his power from Grayskull. Both gray and skull give off strong images of death.[2]

A concerned grandmother told me that she had bought her grandson a He-Man sword. One day while working in the kitchen, she could hear her grandson playing in the back yard. The grandmother was struck with curiousity over the repetition of the words, "by the power of Grayskull, by the power of Grayskull." She stepped out on the back porch where she could see her grandson. He was holding the sword above his head, repeating the phrase over and over. The grandmother told me the boy would not respond to her call. The boy was literally in a trance. She said, "It scared me; I had to shake him back into reality."

Both He-Man and She-Ra get help from the sorceress

which lives in Grayskull. He-Man has also been helped by a wizard named Zodac.[3] (Strangely enough, Zodac is only missing the letter "i," which would make it the word "zodiac.")

What does the Bible say about wizards and sorcerers? Leviticus 19:31 says, *"Regard not them that have familiar spirits, neither seek after wizards, to be defiled by them: I am the LORD your God."*

Just like Simon of old, He-Man claims to be great. Acts 8:9 says, *"But there was a certain man, called Simon, which beforetime in the same city used sorcery, and bewitched the people of Samaria, giving out that himself was some great one."*

The Bible tells us in Revelation 18:23b, *". . . for by thy sorceries were all nations deceived."* This is yet to come, according to prophecy. This is the future—that the nations will be deceived by sorcery, yet that is all you see on television—sorcery and witchcraft. The Bible is true.

She-Ra gets her name from the Egyptian sun god, Ra. Are the producers aware of this? Yes. If you look on the front of her dress, she has a prominent sun symbol on it. She has a unicorn named Spirit for transportation. Unicorns have become very popular. Many people collect them. Some even suggest that unicorns are mentioned in the Bible.

Unicorns are mentioned in the Bible, but the unicorn of the Bible was of the oxen family. The unicorn of the occult and mythology is of the horse family. There are occult book stores named "Unicorn." The unicorn of the occult was only to be approached by a virgin. Virgin worship has strong roots in paganism.

Is it coincidence that the horn of the unicorn protrudes from the center of the forehead? The occultist believes that there is a third eye in the forehead. It is the all-seeing eye, or the eye of knowledge.

She-Ra gives all honor to Grayskull. Who should Christians give honor to? John 5:23 says, *"That all men should honour the Son, even as they honour the Father. He that honoureth not the Son honoureth not the Father which hath sent him."* In 1 Corinthians 10:31 we read, *"Whether therefore ye eat, or drink, or whatsoever ye do, do all to the glory of God."*

Ecology or Theology, You Make the Call

"Who changed the truth of God into a lie, and worshipped and served the creature more than the Creator, who is blessed for ever. Amen." (Rom. 1:25)

I was doing a live radio talk show in Denver, Colorado, when a lady called in very concerned about her daughter. Apparently, her daughter had met a group of people involved in witchcraft and they had convinced her that witchcraft was the true religion.

We prayed for this woman and her daughter. The next night after the meeting a lady and her teenage daughter walked up and identified themselves as the woman and girl we had prayed for the day before.

For over an hour we sat in the auditorium of this church pleading with this girl to turn from paganism. One of her greatest reasons for not coming to Christianity was because Christianity was a religion for men. She told me that the God we served was a God who hated women. See, witchcraft and goddess worship go hand in hand. This girl had been drawn into the worship of witchcraft by being told that God disliked women. Goddess worship is quickly becoming the religion of choice in America. Some have taken the Gaia hypothesis which states that Gaia (or mother) is a living being and that we are all a part of a larger whole. People are now studying ecology as theology. This quote is from *Time* magazine:

> *"To mark Earth Day last week, four women and two men stood on a hilltop outside Mount Horeb, Wisconsin, literally praying to Mother Earth, 'Sacred Earth Power, bring healing to planet Earth,' intoned barefoot Selena Fox, priestess of Circle Sanctuary. Worshippers responded with a crescendo chant, 'Clean soil; clean soil,' then pledged to do a variety of ecological good deeds and joined in a hug. Similar nature worship was part of Earth Day festivals from Boston, where the Goddess Gospel singers performed on the waterfront, to Berkeley, where devotees drummed and sang for a crowd. . . . Despite*

Christianity's centuries of opposition to paganism, some old-line churches are opening up to the Goddess. A witch teaches in an institute at the Roman Catholic Holy Names College in California. A book by two United Methodist pastors proposes experimental Bible readings about the crucifixion that replaces Jesus with Sophia (Wisdom), a name for the divine personality used by Goddess-minded Christians."[1]

Those involved in the feminist movement are referred to as she-ologians instead of theologians. They study sheology instead of theology. Don't get me wrong. I have talked to many people who were concerned with the environment that were not involved in witchcraft. But I have never met a witch that did not believe in Mother Earth. Believe it or not, you can be concerned about the environment without worshipping it.

"Eight lanes of rush hour traffic roared past the witches and warlocks gathered in a downtown park to beg the Earth's forgiveness, here in the world's most polluted city. Antonio Vasquez estimates more than two hundred fifty thousand people practice some form of white or black magic in Mexico, where potions or powers to snare a lover or curse an enemy can be bought in many markets."[2]

Children are being bombarded with "Save the Planet." Cartoons like "Captain Planet" portray Gaia Mother Earth. The cartoon *Fern Gully* taught children that the people who cut down trees are inspired by an evil, demonic presence, and that trees have feelings, too. Are the New Agers teaching children ecology, or is it sheology? The answer to the question is easy. Sheology is coming through loud and clear. Pantheism is the belief that God is in all, and that all is God.

In the book of Exodus, God sent ten plagues on the Egyptian people. Each plague was a direct attack on an Egyptian god. God will one day again unleash His wrath upon the goddess Gaia. Let us look at Revelation 8:7–9, *"The first angel sounded, and there followed hail and fire mingled with blood, and they were cast upon the earth: and the third part of trees was burnt up, and all green grass was burnt up. And the second angel sounded, and as it were a great mountain burning with fire was cast into the sea: and the third part of the sea became blood; And the third part of the creatures which were in the sea, and had life, died; and the third part of the ships were destroyed."*

God will judge the queen of heaven in Revelation 8:12, *"And the fourth angel sounded, and the third part of the sun was smitten, and the third part of the moon, and the third part of the stars; so as the third part of them was darkened, and the day shone not for a third part of it, and the night likewise."*

Even though God is neither male nor female, He is God. The reason we do not pray to a female deity is because Jesus taught us to pray to "Our *Father* who art in heaven." Who twenty years ago, would have ever imagined that people would have a hard time identifying God. America is rapidly moving toward a sexless generation, and, obviously, I am speaking about gender. We have a postal worker instead of a postman. We have a sales person instead of a salesman. Even God comes under attack.

How Do We Know That God Does Not Show Favoritism to Men?

1. He didn't blame Eve; He blamed Adam.
2. If goddess worship is for women and Christianity is a religion for men, then why are there always

more women in church than men?
3. What about the stories of the great women in the
   Bible: Esther, Ruth, Martha, Mary?

Today people are offended by scriptures like these: *"Then
said Jesus to them again, Peace be unto you: as my Father
hath sent me, even so send I you"* (John 20:21). *"For as the
Father hath life in himself; so hath he given to the Son to
have life in himself"* (John 5:26).

Believe it or not, the reading of scriptures such as these
makes some people very angry. I would be labeled a sexist
by them. Others would yell, "Discrimination!" Yes, some of
those who demand equal rights for women would say that
God is a She.

Five Arguments For God Being Our Father Which Art In Heaven, and not our mother

Argument #1: *The Linguistic Argument*—Every time the
Scripture refers to God, it is in the masculine gender, whether
it is Hebrew, Aramaic, or Greek.

Argument #2: *Jesus' Reference to Him*—Jesus refers to
the *Father* over two hundred times during His earthly ministry. (By the way, the same people that say God could be a
female would have no problem believing that Jesus could have
been a homosexual. You see, it is not a sexist view, it is a
perverted view.)

Argument #3: *The Psychological View*—Many psychologists believe that children develop their views of God through
the father image in the home. Usually, if people have a hard
time trusting God, they find out they have had a hard time
believing their fathers first. Obviously, when a person thinks
of a voice speaking to Moses or Noah, he relates more to the
voice of Charlton Heston than he does to that of Farrah
Fawcett.

Argument #4: *The Historical Argument*—You must understand that turning God into a woman is not a new trick for Satan. All that one would have to do is study some of the false gods to find that many wanted to serve female deities. Several examples would be:

1. Asherah, the chief goddess of Tyre; she was known as the Lady of the Sea
2. Ashtoreth, the Canaanite goddess of Baal's lovers
3. Diana, the multibreasted goddess who was believed to be the nursing mother of the other gods
4. Isis

Argument #5: *The Satanic Argument*—While all this debate is going on, one could overlook its author, Satan. That's right. What most people do not know is that Satan is pictured in occult art as a creature having a goat's head, a woman's breast, and animal's legs and finally, cloven hooves.

So maybe they are right. They do serve a female god, but he is not the father of Jesus Christ, nor is he our heavenly Father. He is Satan, who is known as the "god of this world." You see, God is not suffering from an identity crisis. It is the world who has a problem when it cannot identify Him.

Beauty and the Beast

"Be sober, be vigilant; because your adversary the devil, as a roaring lion, walketh about, seeking whom he may devour." (1 Pet. 5:8)

It has been called a classic. It has been called a beautiful love story. Does this story only teach that we should love those things that are not lovely, or is there a deeper meaning? Recently I was at a Christian television station preparing for a special that night. I was challenged by one of the technical people about *Beauty and the Beast*, who said, "I can buy a lot of what you say, but not everything. What could possibly be wrong with *Beauty and the Beast?*"

Here is an excerpt from an actual letter we received:

> *Dear Ones:*
> *Your tape, 14 Things Witches Hope Parents Never Find Out, was very informative. However, I was hoping to hear comments about Beauty and the Beast. The non-Christians, as well as the Christians, have accepted this with arms wide open. Is this so-called masterpiece all good? I have some uncomfortable thoughts.*
>
> *Alice*

First of all, let me assure you that I do not expect everyone to accept everything I say. My wife is my best friend, yet I allow her to disagree with me. And she allows me to disagree with her. But we still love each other. She can be a *beauty*, and I can be a *beast*!

Secondly, this material is not to convert people over to the Benoit School of Philosophy. It is only to make Christian people aware of some entry points Satan may or may not have in your home. With that thought in mind, let us examine how beautiful the "Beast" really is.

Let me complete this story of the young man at the Christian television station. I looked at the gentleman and asked this question: "Is *Beauty and the Beast* fantasy or reality?" The fellow quickly responded, "Pure fantasy." Maybe that would be the exact response you would have made. You must understand that the most dangerous truth is a half-truth. If the devil can mix enough fantasy with enough reality, we will be totally confused.

For example, in the chapter "Satan Is Trolling for Souls," we discussed the incubus spirit that materializes like a man to have sex with women. You say fantasy, yet I've had women tell me they have experienced encounters with these ugly spirits. Genesis 6:1–5 may be a reference to these spirits, *"And it came to pass, when men began to multiply on the face of the earth, and daughters were born unto them, That the sons of God saw the daughters of men that they were fair; and they took them wives of all which they chose. And the LORD said, My spirit shall not always strive with man, for that he also is flesh: yet his days shall be an hundred and twenty years. There were giants in the earth in those days; and also after that, when the sons of God came in unto the daughters of men, and they bare children to them, the same became mighty men which were of old, men of renown. And God saw that the wickedness of man was great in the earth, and that every imagination of the thoughts of his heart was only evil continually."*

Now to answer the question of whether *Beauty and the Beast* is fantasy or reality. To answer that question, I may have to introduce you to a man who lived about six hundred years before Christ. His name was Nebuchadnezzar.

Nebuchadnezzar was the king of Babylon that had Shadrach, Meshach, and Abednego thrown into the fiery furnace. He is mentioned ninety-one times in the Bible. Unlike some kings in the Bible who are obscure, this man was very influential in the lives of the Jewish people.

Even though Nebuchadnezzar was powerful and influential, he was no match for God. Daniel 4:28–34 says, *"All this came upon the king Nebuchadnezzar. At the end of twelve months he walked in the palace of the kingdom of Babylon.*

The king spake, and said, Is not this great Babylon, that I have built for the house of the kingdom by the might of my power, and for the honour of my majesty? While the word was in the king's mouth, there fell a voice from heaven, saying, O king Nebuchadnezzar, to thee it is spoken; The kingdom is departed from thee. And they shall drive thee from men, and thy dwelling shall be with the beasts of the field: they shall make thee to eat grass as oxen, and seven times shall pass over thee, until thou know that the most High ruleth in the kingdom of men, and giveth it to whomsoever he will. The same hour was the thing fulfilled upon Nebuchadnezzar: and he was driven from men, and did eat grass as oxen, and his body was wet with the dew of heaven, till his hairs were grown like eagles' feathers, and his nails like birds' claws. And at the end of the days I Nebuchadnezzar lifted up mine eyes unto heaven, and mine understanding returned unto me, and I blessed the most High, and I praised and honoured him that liveth for ever, whose dominion is an everlasting dominion, and his kingdom is from generation to generation."

Just like Lucifer (see Isa. 14:12–14), Nebuchadnezzar was lifted up by pride. There are two interpretations to these passages:

1. Nebuchadnezzar went insane and lived with the animals.
2. Nebuchadnezzar was transformed into an animal. Those involved with the occult call this transformation "lycanthropy." The scientific term is "boanthropic-mono-maniac."

> *"We realize that men or women—are merely animals without the fur or the feathers. Sometimes the hero is a self-enchanter who can change his shape at will, and is perhaps rather more comfortable as an animal than as a man. (We remember that the*

olympians, particularly Zeus, had a naughty habit of assuming animal shapes in order to descend unsuspected but irresistibly on the objects of their desire. The lovely Helen had to own a swan as her father, and the mighty Minos a bull)."[1]

THE METABOLISM OF THE BODY

In Daniel 4:33 we read, *"The same hour was the thing fulfilled upon Nebuchadnezzar: and he was driven from men, and did eat grass as oxen, and his body was wet with the dew of heaven, till his hairs were grown like eagles' feathers, and his nails like birds' claws."* He did this for seven years. If a person tried to eat grass for seven years, he would die of malnutrition. The human body must be changed. The key to the change may be found in Daniel 5:21, *"And he was driven from the sons of men; and his heart was made like the beasts, and his dwelling was with the wild asses: they fed him with grass like oxen, and his body was wet with the dew of heaven; till he knew that the most high God ruled in the kingdom of men, and that he appointeth over it whomsoever he will."* You see, Nebuchadnezzar had a heart transplant! God gave him the heart of a beast!

Barney

HEY WAIT! I THINK I CAN SEE ... BARNEY!

"Casting down imaginations, and every high thing that exalteth itself against the knowledge of God, and bringing into captivity every thought to the obedience of Christ." (2 Cor. 10:5)

Without a doubt, the most asked question I have is, "What about Barney?" Some at this point will say, "I knew before this man was done that he would even find something wrong with the *Andy Griffith Show*." Well, this time you are wrong. I am not talking about *that* Barney. I am talking about Barney the purple dinosaur. Barney is one of the newest rages among children's programming. He could easily be called a phenomenon in children's television.

Some may ask why Barney is so successful. There are at least two reasons why Barney is so successful.

The void of good things for children today, in a world where every children's program has to do with sorcery, wizards, and mutated turtles. Parents are frustrated! Parents are looking for something safe for their children. So one day they turn on PBS and there are children singing, "I love you, you love me, we're a happy family." Parents are excited to find a program that doesn't have rock and roll and sex as a part of its daily lessons. Finally, something safe for our children to watch is the cry of many Christian parents. But is Barney really safe? That is a question we will explore later.

Barney has a master for a marketing agent. You must understand that Barney is not a tremendous success by accident, but by design. That's right. Barney has a unique way of being marketed. Let me explain:

Small children only respond as they are taught to respond. Have you ever noticed how children are a reflection of you as a parent? Have you ever seen your child's impersonation of you? For example, you shake your finger and crinkle your nose and say, "We don't like rock and roll." One day you see your child playing house in a corner, and all of a sudden you see your child crinkle their little nose and point their little finger, and say, "We don't like rock and roll." They do it exactly the way they were taught. The same principle applies to the marketing of Barney.

You must understand that your child may not love Barney as much as you think. They may have only been taught how to respond to Barney by the children on the program. Every time Barney appears, he is greeted with uncontrolled jubilation from the children. The child has been programmed to respond in jubilation every time he sees Barney, but then parents say, "I don't understand it; my children are crazy about Barney."

Are they really crazy over this purple dinosaur, or are they just impersonating the children on the show? Could your toddler subtly be programmed to believe that if he or she does not love Barney that they would be considered strange? Have you as a parent felt pressure to involve your child in the Barney movement for fear that your child would be rejected if he did not become a Barney fan?

The million-dollar question is, "Is this wrong?" Are children misled by children's products advertised on television? Don't you remember as a child how toys on television did not work exactly the same way at home? Doesn't it make you angry when you see these toy campaigns work your child into a frenzy over something you know is not at all what it seems on television? In essence, marketing is neither right nor wrong in and of itself. Where it becomes right or wrong is the product that they are marketing. Now the question: "Is Barney a totally safe product?"

COULD IT BE POSSIBLE FOR BARNEY TO BECOME A MARKETING TOOL FOR NEW AGE PROPAGANDA?

Barney is a dinosaur. For years the secular humanists have used the dinosaur to prove that this world is millions of years old. Evolution is taught, not creation. The secular humanists have used the dinosaur as a tool to prove there is no God. Has Barney ever given his age? How old did he say he was? We who believe in creation, as opposed to those who believe in evolution, believe that dinosaurs lived on this planet about five or six thousand years ago—not millions of years ago. Barney is not the only dinosaur on PBS. If Barney was not an object lesson for evolution, he would be the only dinosaur on PBS not to be.

The producers of this program would be foolish to put Barney's age up before every program. Barney in and of himself is an object lesson that supports evolution. If the humanists have fought for years to keep creation out of our public schools, should we not fight as hard to keep evolution out of our Christian homes?

Could Barney subtly be promoting guided imagery to children? For those of you who do not know what guided imagery is, I will explain it to you. Guided imagery is a New Age technique of going into your mind in order to find a spirit guide that will help you solve your problems. According to Berit Kjos,

> *"Guided imagery is visualization exercises directed by a teacher or leader. While some merely relax, others produce altered states of consciousness including trance, a sense of astral projections, and connection with a spirit guide."*[1]

In the book *Child Spirit—Children's Experience with God in School*, author Samuel Silverstein shows how easy it is to put children into an altered state of consciousness.

> *"The equilibrium that is needed in the body to make contact with forces from above can occur in children very quickly, even when they are in bed half asleep. It can also happen to them after they say a prayer in church, or when they put their heads down on their school desks, breathe deeply several times,*

relax their bodies, and think of God. If conditions are right, a child in a public school classroom can make this contact with God in about ten to fifteen seconds."[2]

Do not be confused with the constant reference of contacting God. Silverstein, on the back of his book, indicates his belief in the gods of the New Age:

"Enter the secret world of eight-year-olds—a world of pure connection to angels, out-of-body states, balls of light, lightning bolts with little people within, and God! In this delightfully profound book, former science teacher Samuel Silverstein shares with us the results of three years of carefully recorded research performed with his third-grade classes. Revealing with refreshing simplicity the visionary and religious experiences of the children, he then relates them to similar accounts by biblical figures, great saints, and Eastern mysticism. Child Spirit *is a book for the child mystics within each of us and for parents who want to more deeply appreciate the inner world of their children.*"[3]

The book *Child Spirit* was introduced by David Spangler. For those of you who are not familiar with that name, he is one of the leaders of the modern New Age movement. He is quoted as saying,

"No one will enter the New World Order unless he or she makes a pledge to worship Lucifer. No one will enter the New Age unless he will take a Luciferic initiation."[4]

The only thing that really concerns me about Barney is that he becomes an imaginary problem solver. On the program he starts off as a stuffed dinosaur just like your children can buy at the store. Then, all of a sudden, he appears in the imagination of these children. They go on imaginary trips, and he helps the children solve their problems in their imagination. As a matter of fact, on the tape box of every Barney video they say their desire is that Barney will become your child's life-long friend. It is interesting to note that in *Child Spirit* they talk about friends who have materialized for these children.

> *"Children have spiritual friends they talk to whom no one else can see. One girl saw her friend take shape right in front of her out of colored particles."*[5]

These were the same types of particles that one would have seen had they watched the movie *Ghost*. Think about that. When I was growing up I had Mister Green Jeans and Captain Kangaroo, but they are not my life-long friends. Besides that, the Bible tells us to put away childish things. As a Christian parent your child may never come in contact with a New Age teacher, but the majority of the children in our country will. Any good teacher knows the value of visual aids. If a New Age teacher can use Barney as a way to teach an imaginary problem solver, they will do it.

Do I think that Barney is of the devil? No. Do I believe that the devil could use a toy named Barney? Yes. Do I believe that one day Barney will come out on his program wearing New Age jewelry, and praying to the sun god while reading the Satanic Bible and listening to heavy metal music? Absolutely not. You see, it is the little foxes that spoil the grapes.

Sometime ago I heard a story of a missionary who led a woman to the Lord on the mission field. The missionary then set out to reach the husband. The husband seemed to be a nice guy, so every morning the missionary would go to his home and witness to the man while drinking a cup of coffee with him. Not long after this fellowship started, the missionary became very ill. His hair started to fall out and he started losing weight. Despite the many tests run on him, this strange illness could not be explained. The man was slowly dying. One day he went to see a doctor who had lived among these people for a long time. The doctor took one look at him and asked him if he had been around rat poison. The missionary assured him he had not, but the doctor concluded that he had been poisoned.

What had happened is that every morning when he went to visit this lady's husband, he put small doses of rat poison in the missionary's cup. So, the sickness came gradually, not all of a sudden. That is the same way the devil does it. He will not give your children heavy doses of New Age and occult philosophies. He will just give them small doses until one day, they are slowly destroyed. The devil is very patient.

Finally, a story that was told to me by a missionary may show the subtlety of Barney. This missionary said she knew nothing about Barney until one day her two-year-old daughter saw Barney on the *TV Guide*. Her daughter ran over to the *TV Guide* saying, "Barney, Barney." This was confusing to the mother because she did not have a clue who or what Barney was. She later found out that her daughter's Sunday school teacher was playing Barney videos for the children instead of teaching them the Bible.

I wonder how many other Sunday school teachers play Barney on Sunday morning to mesmerize the children instead of teaching them the Word of God. When you consider how few parents have devotions with their children, when you consider how little Bible is taught to children, when our churches have to have a purple dinosaur substitute teach for our Sunday school teachers, something is wrong! Sunday school is a time to feed these little sheep. God help the Sunday school teacher who sees Sunday morning as a baby sit-ting job instead of an opportunity to mold young minds for Christ.

Without doing an exam, a doctor cannot look at you and tell you where you are hurting or why you are sick. A building inspector cannot just look at your house to see if you have termites. Be careful about saying that you do not see anything wrong with Barney unless you have studied it by using objective analysis. *Do not judge a book by its cover!*

Situation Ethics and Those Who Have None

OK CHILDREN, I WANT YOU TO THINK OF SOMEONE YOU REALLY ADMIRE...

"Woe unto them that call evil good, and good evil; that put darkness for light, and light for darkness; that put bitter for sweet, and sweet for bitter! Woe unto them that are wise in their own eyes, and prudent in their own sight!" (Isa. 5:20–21)

Here is a situation. Your friend's daughter has fallen in love with a young man. You are concerned about this girl because of these particular things you know about the boy:

1. He is a thief. That's right. He has nearly gotten caught stealing several times by security at the local grocery story.
2. He is a cute boy, but he doesn't live at home. He finds places to sleep in the city.
3. He is at this time unemployed and has dropped out of school.
4. He also practices magic. He is into white magic and only does good things for people. It has been rumored that he can levitate (that means he can suspend his body in mid-air).
5. He is very likeable, but you have to watch him. He can lie like a rug and you would believe every word he says. He is clever and very streetwise. There is still more you ought to know about this young man.
6. He is a Muslim. He comes from the Islamic faith. (By the way, Muslims are not very tolerant to Christianity.)
7. Your friend unknowingly has encouraged his daughter to admire this young man.
8. Finally, you ought to know his name. He simply goes by the name *Aladdin*.

It is amazing how by isolating the person of Aladdin from the music and story, you realize he may not be the person you want your young son or daughter to admire. Situation ethics has, for years, been taught in our educational system. Teachers often test the child's thinking by trying to get that child to answer only one question. Is it right to do wrong if it turns out right?

Sometime ago they renamed the class from "situational

ethics" to "values clarification." This class brought Christian leaders to arms. Why? What is wrong with teaching values to students? The problem with this program was that Christian children were being taught values by those who didn't have any.

Humanist teachers who believe that homosexuality is normal make Christian children look like bigots if they do not agree. Humanist teachers who believe in premarital sex, abortion, and atheism make children with homespun values look like outcasts if they believe in saving their virginity, saving babies, or saving their faith. Most Christian parents would wholeheartedly agree that those without values should leave our children with values alone. According to the *The Encyclopedia on Witches and Witchcraft*:

> *"In Arab and Muslim folklore, the djinn are de-mons, usually ugly and evil, who possess supernatu-ral powers and serve those who know the correct magic. The western term is GENIE! In pre-Islamic folklore, the djinn roamed the deserts and wilderness. They were malicious. Though usually invisible, they had the power to take on any shape—insect, animal, or human. They were adopted into Islamic lore and modified; some were allowed to become beautiful and good-natured. Solomon tamed them and became their ruler with the help of his magic ring, which was set with a gem—probably a diamond—that had a living force of its own and protected him from evil. He car-ried them on his back when he traveled and directed them to make statues, gardens, and palaces. Djinn appear in tales such as* Aladdin's Lamp *in* Arabian Nights, *in which they carry out the wishes of a master who learns the magic that will command them. There are five kinds of djinn of varying degrees of power.*

The most important individual djinnee is Iblis, the prince of darkness. "[1]

Hollywood has been accused of a lot of things, but having values is not one of them. Why, don't you know that Hollywood has the best? Yes, they have the best advocates for homosexuals. They have the best proponents for abortion. They have the best humanists in the country. And these actors or teachers will work hard to change your child's value system so that they will rebel against the parent.

It is never right to do wrong to do right. Yes, everybody likes to see a reformed life; yes, everyone wants to see bad go good. But have we gone overboard in making Robin Hood-type heroes for our children?

I can understand bad becoming good through the power of Jesus Christ. By the time I was fifteen I was in reform school for possession of drugs. When I was released, I was reformed but not transformed.

What we need today are heroes who have been transformed and not necessarily reformed. We need heroes like Corri Ten Boom, the author of *The Hiding Place*, Adonirum Judson, and Hudson Taylor. My heroes are not those who overcame great sins, but instead those who overcame great temptations. There are millions of godly people who have never tasted hard liquor. There are millions of people who sit in our churches who have said "no" to drugs and extra-marital affairs. There are many in our churches who have such a great testimony because they never wandered out into the depths of sin. They are the heroes. This chapter should be for every godly parent who are heroes to their children. My desire for my children is not that they would do bad and then come back into the fold. My desire is that my children would always have Jesus Christ as their hero.

Bereavement and Braindead

"Children, obey your parents in the Lord: for this is right. Honour thy father and mother; which is the first commandment with promise; That it may be well with thee, and thou mayest live long on the earth. And, ye fathers, provoke not your children to wrath: but bring them up in the nurture and admonition of the Lord." (Eph. 6:1–4)

It was youth camp at 6:59 p.m. This means total pandemonium before the evening service! The camp director calls the troops together for an evening of fun and fellowship. As always, you give the campers group games or activities before the preaching, so this night was no exception. Six teens were selected to play a *Name That Tune* type of game.

The first tune was easy—"The Theme to Gilligan's Island." Then came, "The Theme to Green Acres," and a few of the older television sitcoms. Then out of nowhere came a tune that I had never heard, but before six notes were played, everyone on the panel jumped to their feet. The team members on the sideline were jumping up and down with their hands up like a bunch of first-graders who had to really go to the bathroom. This puzzled me. How could a whole Christian youth camp know a theme song that I had never heard? I was not in a state of bewilderment very long before a young man said, *"Beavis and B-head!"* His team was ecstatic that he was able to get the answer correct. When I first heard the answer, I didn't want to congratulate the boy. I was confused because the camp director didn't reprimand the game leader for putting that song in his program, and the teen was not reprimanded for using profanity.

Beavis and B-head is an animated program on MTV. They have taken their place in line in what seems to be the trend. This is how *Newsweek* describes these two degenerates:

> *"The boys are Beavis and Butthead, two animated miscreants whose adventures at the low end of the food chain are currently the most popular program on MTV. Caught in the ungainly nadir of adolescence, they are not nice boys. They torture animals, they harass girls, and sniff paint thinner. They like to burn things. They have a really insidious laugh: huh-huh-huh-huh. They are the spiritual descendants of the*

semi-sentiment teens from Wayne's World *and* Bill and Ted's Excellent Adventure, *only dumber and meaner. The downward spiral of the living white male surely ends here: in a little pimple named Butthead whose idea of an idea is, 'Hey, Beavis, let's go over to Stuart's house and light one in his cat's butt.'"*[1]

As a matter of fact, MTV had to move this program to late night after a young boy set his house on fire, allegedly killing his younger sibling, yet MTV has vowed they are going to start an anti-violence campaign. Another instance of how they promote violence is a story of two girls in Ohio who were watching these two characters as they tried to set fire to each other's hair by using a match and the spray from an aerosol can. The girls admitted they saw the two and wanted to see if they could do it, too. How can MTV in good conscience say they are against violence when their number-one program, *B&B*, promotes it?

MTV's bottom line may be money, but the devil's bottom line is mayhem. MTV's bottom line may be the all-mighty dollar, but the devil's bottom line is fury. MTV's bottom line may be cash flow, but the devil's bottom line is corruption flowing.

Judy McGrath, MTV's president and creative director, may claim she wants to declare war on violence, but it is hard to believe. **It would be easier for me to believe that . . .**

1. Jesse Jackson wants to be the keynote speaker at a convention for white supremacy.
2. Ted Kennedy wants to build a summer home next to the Chappaquiddick.
3. Al Gore wants to work as a stump grinder in the rain forest.
4. Ted Turner and Jane Fonda want to give Jerry Falwell a billion dollars.

5. Bill and Hillary Clinton want Rush Limbaugh to spend a week with them at Camp David.
6. Madonna wants to do a concert to raise money for pro-life.
7. Madeline Murray O'Hare wants to donate her time to pass out Bibles for the Gideons.
8. R.J. Reynolds is buying stock in patches that help people stop smoking.
9. Saddam Hussein wants to have breakfast with Norman Schwartzkoff.
10. Dan Quayle wants to become a regular on the "Murphy Brown Show."
11. David Koresh was for gun control.

As you can see, I have a difficult time believing that MTV—with its reputation for promoting violence—is going to tell our youth to stop violence. Matthew 24:37–38 says, *"But as the days of Noe were, so shall also the coming of the Son of man be. For as in the days that were before the flood they were eating and drinking, marrying and giving in marriage, until the day that Noe entered into the ark."* The days of Noah were times of unfaithfulness and self-indulgence, but violence was one of the main reasons for God's judgment. Genesis 6:11–13 says, *"The earth also was corrupt before God, and the earth was filled with violence. And God looked upon the earth, and, behold, it was corrupt; for all flesh had corrupted his way upon the earth. And God said unto Noah, The end of all flesh is come before me; for the earth is filled with violence through them; and, behold, I will destroy them with the earth."*

Did you know that *B&B* have an album? It is entitled *The Beavis and Butthead Experience.* Here are some songs from that album:

1. *I Hate Myself and Want to Die*, performed by Nir-

vana (Nirvana is a perfect state of blissfulness. It would be equivalent to Heaven for Christians. Nirvana is directly linked to reincarnation.)

2. *Looking Down the Barrel of a Gun*, performed by Anthrax

3. *99 Ways to Die*, performed by Megadeth

4. *I Am Hell*, performed by White Zombie

5. *Search and Destroy*, performed by the Red Hot Chili Peppers

Our society is definitely on a downward spiral when our families laugh at violence, death, and destruction.

Yin and Yang
Made Plain

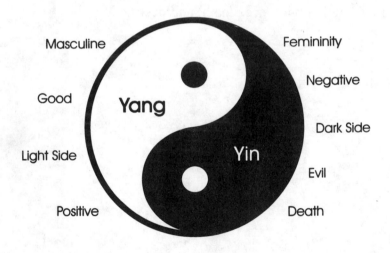

Yin-Yang—Two opposite but complementary energies of any unified whole: positive/negative, male/female, light/dark, strong/weak. The two balancing polarities of the universal force which infuses all things. Symbolized by a circle divided by a serpentine line. Yin is the black side with the white "eye," and Yang is the white side with the black "eye." **(Berit Kjos, *Your Child and the New Age*, p. 120)**

They are an inseparable pair. They find themselves in everything from martial arts to fashion design. Yet most Americans do not know the theory behind the yin and yang. The yin and yang theory gets its roots from ancient China.

According to the belief of the yin and yang, it enters the body at birth and departs the body at death. This theory postulates that good and evil precede from the same force. This basic precept comes from Taoism (pronounced "dowism"). Tao means "the way."

"The most important aspect of Taoistic philosophy to consider when discussing modern cults is the dualistic view of opposites known as yin and yang. These two essences are said to symbolize the complementary nature of all forces in the universe which seem to be diametric."[1]

It is interesting to note that many involved in witchcraft and feminism have no problem with the yin-yang theory. Yet according to the teaching of the yin and yang, it has some very chauvinistic views.

"Yang is the positive force of good, light, life, and masculinity. Yin is the negative essence of evil, death, and femininity. All matter is said to contain both yin and yang and orderly affairs are possible only when these two qualities exist in a state of proper equilibrium."[2]

While Christianity may be considered a prejudiced religion against women, the New Age movement boasts at its attraction for women. The basic premise for the yin and the yang could be called "dualistic theology." That is the good and evil precede from the same source. These two forces by battling one another balance out. According to *Eerdman's Handbook to the World's Religions*, yin-yang is also accredited with seasons. *"Yin and yang produce the elements and the cycle of the seasons. "*[3] The seasons are very important in pagan worship. If a person believed in yin and yang, they would easily accept:

● "white" magic and "black" magic.
● the good side of the force or the dark side of the force, mentioned in *Star Wars.*
● that God represents the good side, and that the devil represents the dark side of the force, both stemming from the same source.

Here are some direct conflicts that Christianity has with Taoism:

Taoism teaches that yin and yang enter at birth and leave at death. According to Genesis 2:7, *"And the LORD God formed man of the dust of the ground, and breathed into his nostrils the breath of life; and man became a living soul."* God breathed the breath of life into Adam. He did not put yin and yang into operation. By the way, Adam did not have good and evil working together in him. Sin did not enter the human race until after the fall of Genesis 3.

Satan, or Lucifer, and God are two forces working against one another.

SATAN

Satan is a real person, not a force. Isaiah 14:12 says, *"How art thou fallen from heaven, O Lucifer, son of the morning! how art thou cut down to the ground, which didst weaken the nations!"*

He has real intelligence. Isaiah 14:13 says, *"For thou hast said in thine heart. . . . "*

He has a real will. We read in Isaiah 14:13-14, *"I will ascend into heaven, I will exalt my throne above the stars of God: I will sit also upon the mount of the congregation, in the sides of the north: I will ascend above the heights of the clouds; I will be like the most High."*

He has a real destiny. Isaiah 14:15 says, *"Yet thou shalt be brought down to hell, to the sides of the pit."*

He has a real desire. We read in Luke 22:31, *"And the Lord said, Simon, Simon, behold, Satan hath desired to have you, that he may sift you as wheat"*

He has a real plan. *"Lest Satan should get an advantage of us: for we are not ignorant of his devices"* (2 Cor. 2:11).

GOD

God has creating powers. In Genesis 1:1 we read, *"In the beginning God created the heaven and the earth."*

He can speak in an audible voice. He spoke to Moses and in Exodus 4:1 we read: *"And Moses answered and said, But, behold, they will not believe me, nor hearken unto my voice: for they will say, The LORD hath not appeared unto thee."* He spoke to the people at Jesus' baptism. We read in Matthew 3:17, *"And lo a voice from heaven, saying, This is my beloved Son, in whom I am well pleased."*

He answers prayers. Jesus taught His disciples to pray, "Our Father." In Matthew 6:9 we read, *"After this manner therefore pray ye: Our Father which art in heaven, Hallowed be thy name."* Of the disciples we read in Acts 4:31, *"And when they had prayed, the place was shaken where they were assembled together; and they were all filled with the Holy Ghost, and they spake the word of God with boldness."*

God has a plan for the devil. Revelation 20:9–10 says, *"And they went up on the breadth of the earth, and compassed the camp of the saints about, and the beloved city: and fire came down from God out of heaven, and devoured them. And the devil that deceived them was cast into the lake of fire and brimstone, where the beast and the false prophet are, and shall be tormented day and night for ever and ever."*

Taoism teaches that it is the way; Christ taught that

He was the way. We read in John 14:6, *"Jesus saith unto him, I am the way, the truth, and the life: no man cometh unto the Father, but by me."*

Seven Things Parents Can Do to Prevent Their Children From Getting Involved In Witchcraft

"Finally, my brethren, be strong in the Lord, and in the power of his might. Put on the whole armour of God, that ye may be able to stand against the wiles of the devil." (Eph. 6:10–11)

1. If your child starts having an infatuation with death or drawing skulls, be willing to have open lines of communication. It may be dangerous, but you need to find out where they are getting their information.
2. If your child starts fantasizing with witchcraft or sorcery (like the boy who said, "By the power of Grayskull") that is very dangerous.
3. Avoid cartoons with wizards or sorcerers, such as: Smurfs, He-Man, as well as the Care Bears. (Care Bears get their power from the center of their stomachs, which is Hindu teaching.)
4. Avoid movies that have witches, good or bad.
5. Be aware that some teachers in the public school system may be targeting your child. Know your child's teacher and what he/she is teaching your child.
6. Know your child's friends and the homes they come from.
7. Do not turn your child's bedroom into a haven for the occult. Be careful of radios, tape players, televisions, phones, etc. You know, it used to be that you sent a child to his room for punishment; now that same child goes into his room as an escape hatch. They will stay there for hours and hours. Sometimes you can lose your children because when they are in that room, they are escaping from reality, and that is a danger sign even toward committing suicide.

Twenty-Seven Admonitions

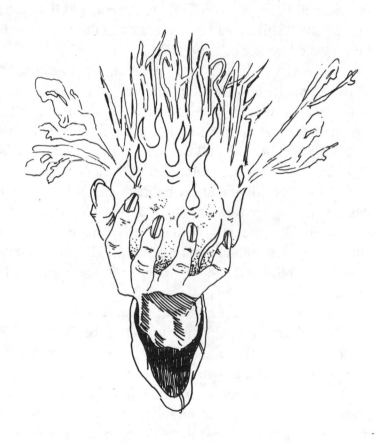

"And many that believed came, and confessed, and showed their deeds. Many of them also which used curious arts brought their books together, and burned them before all men: and they counted the price of them, and found it fifty thousand pieces of silver." (Acts 19:18–19)

1. **Take Satan's tools seriously.** *"Be sober, be vigilant; because your adversary the devil, as a roaring lion, walketh about, seeking whom he may devour"* (1 Pet. 5:8). The Bible says to "be sober." Do you know what that means? To be serious. Did you know that there is a serious problem with mountain lions coming down from the California mountains into certain housing developments? The lions are becoming accustomed to having people around them, and they are attacking small children. I saw a picture of a little girl who had been mauled by one of these lions.

As I was watching a news program one evening, they showed a man who was taking a picture of his child and his wife standing in front of a bush. They could not have been ten feet from that bush. After the man took the picture, they grabbed the child and walked away. What was strange was that when they developed the picture, you could see in the bush a mountain lion just laying there camouflaged by the bush. It was scary to know that the lion was seated there, waiting for the parents to walk away. It was his natural instinct to want to capture and eat that child. That mountain lion would not have had any remorse in tearing that child apart.

When a lion attacks a herd of animals in the wild, many times it scatters the adults in order to prey on the young, defenseless calves. Those animals that run in packs and fight together have a better chance of not being attacked by a lion.

When I saw that program I thought, "Isn't that what the Scripture says? 'Be sober, be vigilant; because your adversary the devil, as a roaring lion, walketh about, seeking whom he may devour.'" He is hoping he can separate you from your children so that he can devour them. Do not take lightly Satan's tools.

2. **Ask God to forgive you for any abomination you have brought into your home.** *"If we confess our sins, he is*

faithful and just to forgive us our sins, and to cleanse us from all unrighteousness" (1 John 1:9).

3. **Realize we are in a warfare.** *"Finally, my brethren, be strong in the Lord, and in the power of his might. Put on the whole armour of God, that ye may be able to stand against the wiles of the devil"* (Eph. 6:10–11).

4. **Understand that our enemy is spiritual.** *"For we wrestle not against flesh and blood, but against principalities, against powers, against the rulers of the darkness of this world, against spiritual wickedness in high places"* (Eph. 6:12).

5. **Know what your armor is.** *"Wherefore take unto you the whole armour of God, that ye may be able to withstand in the evil day, and having done all, to stand. Stand therefore, having your loins girt about with truth, and having on the breastplate of righteousness; And your feet shod with the preparation of the gospel of peace; Above all, taking the shield of faith, wherewith ye shall be able to quench all the fiery darts of the wicked. And take the helmet of salvation, and the sword of the Spirit, which is the word of God: Praying always with all prayer and supplication in the Spirit, and watching thereunto with all perseverance and supplication for all saints"* (Eph. 6:13-18).

6. **Understand that you do not have to fear the devil when you are a spirit-controlled Christian.** *"For God hath not given us the spirit of fear; but of power, and of love, and of a sound mind"* (2 Tim. 1:7).

If fear of the Lord is the beginning of wisdom, then fear of the devil is the beginning of ignorance. The Bible tells us in 2 Corinthians 2:11 to be not ignorant of Satan's devices, lest he deceive us. In Isaiah 12:2 we read, *"Behold, God is my salvation; I will trust, and not be afraid: for the LORD JEHOVAH is my strength and my song; he also is become my salvation."*

Do you know why we have fears? It is because we cannot see the spirit world. But God can see the spirit world, so why should we be afraid if our heavenly Father knows what is going on? I think about a story in 2 Kings 6:15–16. The king of Syria was trying to ambush the king of Israel. Syria would set traps, but Israel never fell into them because Elisha the prophet knew exactly where the traps were. God had let him know. Then one day the king of Syria said, "I am going to get this prophet." He sent all of his troops out to surround the city of Dothan. In verses 15–16 we read, *"And when the servant of the man of God was risen early, and gone forth, behold, an host compassed the city both with horses and chariots. And his servant said unto him, Alas, my master! how shall we do? And he answered, Fear not: for they that be with us are more than they that be with them."*

I can see this servant looking around and saying, "I don't know what you are talking about. 'There are more with us than them' . . . there are only two of us." Verse 17 says, *"And Elisha prayed, and said, LORD, I pray thee, open his eyes, that he may see. And the LORD opened the eyes of the young man; and he saw: and, behold, the mountain was full of horses and chariots of fire round about Elisha."*

When we get a glimpse of God's power, we should not have to be afraid of the devil and his crowd. I have heard that witches have joined fundamental Bible-believing churches in order to destroy the congregation. Do you know why a witch or demon would feel comfortable in a church? When our churches are loaded with witchcraft, our church members are bringing trolls to church, and our Sunday school teachers are showing *The Little Mermaid* in church, it is no wonder witches feel so comfortable there.

If there were people who loved God, hated the devil, and were filled with the Holy Spirit, the church would be so strong that a demon would not feel comfortable there. I used to have a lot of people approach me who were Satanists. They came to our services, and they would holler and scream. But I think the devil wised up, because all these people coming to our services were getting saved. When they see the power of God, it can change their life.

You know a demon should be more afraid of us than we are of it. If we love Jesus Christ and Christ dwells in us the Bible says there are angels encamped around us. They are encamped around me, the pastor, the youth director, and the music director. Do you think a demon would feel comfortable there?

I have also heard that witches pray. Have you ever heard of a witch praying for the fall of the pastors of America? I can tell you that it is not the prayers of witches that are doing it; it is the prayerlessness of the church. I don't want to give praise to a witch. My God answers my prayers. If you say that a pastor fell because of the prayers of a witch, then you are saying that they get more prayers answered than we do. The Bible tells us that greater is He that is in us, than he that is in the world. We don't have to worry about that.

Other scriptures that tell us not to be afraid include: *". . . The LORD is my light and my salvation; whom shall I fear? the LORD is the strength of my life; of whom shall I be afraid?"* (Ps. 27:1). *"There is no fear in love; but perfect love casteth out fear: because fear hath torment. He that feareth is not made perfect in love"* (1 John 4:18).

Do you realize that when you do not trust in Jesus Christ, you will be afraid? By the way, I am not telling you these stories to keep you up all night looking under your bed for demons. I am telling you, as a child of God, that you have authority over demons if you believe you have a greater God than they have.

7. Claim the power and authority you have in Christ. *"Ye are of God, little children, and have overcome them:*

because greater is he that is in you, than he that is in the world" (1 John 4:4). *"Submit yourselves therefore to God. Resist the devil, and he will flee from you"* (Jam. 4:7). *"In whom we have redemption through his blood, even the forgiveness of sins"* (Col. 1:14).

8. **Don't give the devil a foothold.** *"Neither give place to the devil"* (Eph. 4:27).

9. **Remember, we cannot fight Satan in our own strength and power.** *"For the weapons of our warfare are not carnal, but mighty through God to the pulling down of strong holds"* (2 Cor. 10:4). We do not have *Ghostbuster* guns; we have the power of God to knock down the devil.

10. **Remember, Christ has already overcome.** *"Nay, in all these things we are more than conquerors through him that loved us"* (Rom. 8:37).

11. **Don't say, "What I don't know can't hurt me."** There are people who will not come to my seminars because they are afraid that what they know they may be accountable for. If I saw a child playing with a bottle of strychnine and told his parents, the parent cannot say, "Oh, he doesn't even know what that is; therefore it won't hurt him." If the child consumes the strychnine, he will die just as if he had committed suicide.

Remember, don't say, "What I don't know can't hurt me." What you don't know can destroy you! (2 Cor. 2:11).

12. **Be careful of your fellowship with the ungodly.** *"And have no fellowship with the unfruitful works of darkness, but rather reprove them"* (Eph. 5:11).

13. **Fight the good fight.** *"Fight the good fight of faith, lay hold on eternal life, whereunto thou art also called, and hast professed a good profession before many witnesses"* (1 Tim. 6:12).

14. **Know the difference between truth and error.** *"Beloved, believe not every spirit, but try the spirits whether they*

are of God: because many false prophets are gone out into the world. Hereby know ye the Spirit of God: Every spirit that confesseth that Jesus Christ is come in the flesh is of God: And every spirit that confesseth not that Jesus Christ is come in the flesh is not of God: and this is that spirit of antichrist, whereof ye have heard that it should come; and even now already is it in the world. Ye are of God, little children, and have overcome them: because greater is he that is in you, than he that is in the world. They are of the world: therefore speak they of the world, and the world heareth them. We are of God: he that knoweth God heareth us; he that is not of God heareth not us. Hereby know we the spirit of truth, and the spirit of error" (1 John 4:1–6).

15. **Don't be carnal-minded.** *"For to be carnally minded is death; but to be spiritually minded is life and peace. Because the carnal mind is enmity against God: for it is not subject to the law of God, neither indeed can be"* (Rom. 8:6–7).

16. **Avoid the works of the flesh.** *"Now the works of the flesh are manifest, which are these; Adultery, fornication, uncleanness, lasciviousness, Idolatry, witchcraft, hatred, variance, emulations, wrath, strife, seditions, heresies, Envyings, murders, drunkenness, revellings, and such like: of the which I tell you before, as I have also told you in time past, that they which do such things shall not inherit the kingdom of God"* (Gal. 5:19–21).

17. **You can recover your children.** *"And that they may recover themselves out of the snare of the devil, who are taken captive by him at his will"* (2 Tim. 2:26).

18. **Don't let the world steal your love.** *"Love not the world, neither the things that are in the world. If any man love the world, the love of the Father is not in him. For all that is in the world, the lust of the flesh, and the lust of the eyes, and the pride of life, is not of the Father, but is of the*

world" (1 John 2:15–16).

19. **Don't try to imitate the world.** *"And be not conformed to this world: but be ye transformed by the renewing of your mind, that ye may prove what is that good, and acceptable, and perfect, will of God"* (Rom. 12:2).

20. **Know you can overcome the world.** *"For whatsoever is born of God overcometh the world: and this is the victory that overcometh the world, even our faith. Who is he that overcometh the world, but he that believeth that Jesus is the Son of God?"* (1 John 5:4–5).

21. **Know that our weapon is the Word.** *"For the word of God is quick, and powerful, and sharper than any twoedged sword, piercing even to the dividing asunder of soul and spirit, and of the joints and marrow, and is a discerner of the thoughts and intents of the heart"* (Heb. 4:12).

22. **You can't fight the devil alone.** *"Yet Michael the archangel, when contending with the devil he disputed about the body of Moses, durst not bring against him a railing accusation, but said, The Lord rebuke thee"* (Jude 9).

23. **Pray for your children's eyes to be opened.** *"To open their eyes, and to turn them from darkness to light, and from the power of Satan unto God, that they may receive forgiveness of sins, and inheritance among them which are sanctified by faith that is in me"* (Acts 26:18).

24. **Satan can possess children.** *"And he asked his father, How long is it ago since this came unto him? And he said, Of a child"* (Mark 9:21). And because children can possibly be possessed, we need to keep these objects away from our children. We need to pray and protect our children from them.

25. **Christ can protect a believer.** *". . . but he that is begotten of God keepeth himself, and that wicked one toucheth him not"* (1 John 5:18).

26. **Some demons will be removed only through prayer**

and fasting. *"And he said unto them, This kind can come forth by nothing, but by prayer and fasting"* (Mark 9:29).

27. **Remember, God's angels will protect you.** *"Are they not all ministering spirits, sent forth to minister for them who shall be heirs of salvation?"* (Heb. 1:14).

I trust that these words have been an encouragement to you, and I hope that through reading this book we need not fear the devil, but that we need to fear God, understanding that He has great power and will protect us and our families.

References to Victory

"Jesus answered them, Verily, verily, I say unto you, Whosoever committeth sin is the servant of sin. And the servant abideth not in the house for ever: but the Son abideth ever. If the Son therefore shall make you free, ye shall be free indeed." **(John 8:34–36)**

Should we be afraid of the devil? *"Ye are of God, little children, and have overcome them: because greater is he that is in you, than he that is in the world"* (1 John 4:4).

Why should I fight this battle? *"Fight the good fight of faith, lay hold on eternal life, whereunto thou art also called, and hast professed a good profession before many witnesses"* (1 Tim. 6:12).

Are demons active today? *"For we wrestle not against flesh and blood, but against principalities, against powers, against the rulers of the darkness of this world, against spiritual wickedness in high places"* (Eph. 6:12).

Does a Christian fight the battle by himself? *"Likewise also these filthy dreamers defile the flesh, despise dominion, and speak evil of dignities. Yet Michael the archangel, when contending with the devil he disputed about the body of Moses, durst not bring against him a railing accusation, but said, The Lord rebuke thee"* (Jude 8–9).

THE FLESH

Can a carnal-minded Christian be at peace? *"For to be carnally minded is death; but to be spiritually minded is life and peace. Because the carnal mind is enmity against God: for it is not subject to the law of God, neither indeed can be"* (Rom. 8:6–7).

Can we trust our heart? *"For out of the heart proceed evil thoughts, murders, adulteries, fornications, thefts, false witness, blasphemies"* (Matt. 15:19).

"For from within, out of the heart of men, proceed evil thoughts, adulteries, fornications, murders, Thefts, covetousness, wickedness, deceit, lasciviousness, an evil eye, blasphemy, pride, foolishness: All these evil things come from within, and defile the man" (Mark 7:21–23).

Where did sin come from? *"Wherefore, as by one man*

sin entered into the world, and death by sin; and so death passed upon all men, for that all have sinned" (Rom. 5:12).

How can a person be free from sin's hold? *"For if by one man's offence death reigned by one; much more they which receive abundance of grace and of the gift of righteousness shall reign in life by one, Jesus Christ"* (Rom. 5:17).

Should we give place to the devil? *"Neither give place to the devil"* (Eph. 4:27).

What are the works of the flesh? *"Now the works of the flesh are manifest, which are these; Adultery, fornication, uncleanness, lasciviousness, Idolatry, witchcraft, hatred, variance, emulations, wrath, strife, seditions, heresies, Envyings, murders, drunkenness, revellings, and such like: of the which I tell you before, as I have also told you in time past, that they which do such things shall not inherit the kingdom of God"* (Gal. 5:19–21).

What are the fruits of the Spirit? *"But the fruit of the Spirit is love, joy, peace, longsuffering, gentleness, goodness, faith, Meekness, temperance: against such there is no law"* (Gal. 5:22–23).

What should we as Christians do to the flesh? *"And they that are Christ's have crucified the flesh with the affections and lusts. If we live in the Spirit, let us also walk in the Spirit"* (Gal. 5:24-25).

Should a Christian debate with endless questions? *"But foolish and unlearned questions avoid, knowing that they do gender strifes"* (2 Tim. 2:23).

Does the devil have a trap set for you? *"And that they may recover themselves out of the snare of the devil, who are taken captive by him at his will"* (2 Tim. 2:26).

Can Satan hinder you? *"Ye did run well; who did hinder you that ye should not obey the truth?"* (Gal. 5:7).

Is there a war between the flesh and the spirit? *"For the flesh lusteth against the Spirit, and the Spirit against the* *flesh: and these are contrary the one to the other: so that ye cannot do the things that ye would"* (Gal. 5:17).

How can one overcome the lust of the flesh? *"This I say then, Walk in the Spirit, and ye shall not fulfil the lust of the flesh"* (Gal. 5:16).

Are Christians dead to sin? *"Likewise reckon ye also yourselves to be dead indeed unto sin, but alive unto God through Jesus Christ our Lord"* (Rom. 6:11).

What are the benefits of being crucified with Christ? *"I am crucified with Christ: nevertheless I live; yet not I, but Christ liveth in me: and the life which I now live in the flesh I live by the faith of the Son of God, who loved me, and gave himself for me"* (Gal. 2:20).

Can a man be free of sin? *"Knowing this, that our old man is crucified with him, that the body of sin might be destroyed, that henceforth we should not serve sin. For he that is dead is freed from sin"* (Rom. 6:6–7).

What will the love of this world do to our love for God? *"Love not the world, neither the things that are in the world. If any man love the world, the love of the Father is not in him. For all that is in the world, the lust of the flesh, and the lust of the eyes, and the pride of life, is not of the Father, but is of the world"* (1 John 2:15-16)

Will the world love you? *"If ye were of the world, the world would love his own: but because ye are not of the world, but I have chosen you out of the world, therefore the world hateth you"* (John 15:19).

How do Christians avoid the darkness of this world? *"Then Jesus said unto them, Yet a little while is the light with you. Walk while ye have the light, lest darkness come upon you: for he that walketh in darkness knoweth not whither he goeth. While ye have light, believe in the light, that ye may be the children of light. These things spake Jesus, and departed, and did hide himself from them"* (John 12:35-36).

What are the three steps to overcoming the world?
"And he said to them all, If any man will come after me, let him deny himself, and take up his cross daily, and follow me" (Luke 9:23).

What two things does Christ promise to do for the believer?

A. Keep them

B. Pray for them

"I have manifested thy name unto the men which thou gavest me out of the world: thine they were, and thou gavest them me; and they have kept thy word. . . . I pray for them: I pray not for the world, but for them which thou hast given me; for they are thine" (John 17:6,9).

Does Christ make provision for His own? *"I have given them thy word; and the world hath hated them, because they are not of the world, even as I am not of the world. I pray not that thou shouldest take them out of the world, but that thou shouldest keep them from the evil. They are not of the world, even as I am not of the world"* (John 17:14-16).

Should we look like the world to win the world? *"And be not conformed to this world: but be ye transformed by the renewing of your mind, that ye may prove what is that good, and acceptable, and perfect, will of God"* (Rom. 12:2).

How will the world try to trap you? *"Beware lest any man spoil you through philosophy and vain deceit, after the tradition of men, after the rudiments of the world, and not after Christ"* (Col. 2:8).

Should we test the spirits? *"Beloved, believe not every spirit, but try the spirits whether they are of God: because many false prophets are gone out into the world"* (1 John 4:1).

What is our advantage over the world? *"For whatsoever is born of God overcometh the world: and this is the victory that overcometh the world, even our faith. Who is he* *that overcometh the world, but he that believeth that Jesus is the Son of God?"* (1 John 5:4–5).

What is our weapon? *"For the word of God is quick, and powerful, and sharper than any twoedged sword, piercing even to the dividing asunder of soul and spirit, and of the joints and marrow, and is a discerner of the thoughts and intents of the heart"* (Heb. 4:12).

SATAN'S BACKGROUND

"Son of man, take up a lamentation upon the king of Tyrus, and say unto him, Thus saith the Lord GOD; Thou sealest up the sum, full of wisdom, and perfect in beauty. Thou hast been in Eden the garden of God; every precious stone was thy covering, the sardius, topaz, and the diamond, the beryl, the onyx, and the jasper, the sapphire, the emerald, and the carbuncle, and gold: the workmanship of thy tabrets and of thy pipes was prepared in thee in the day that thou wast created. Thou art the anointed cherub that covereth; and I have set thee so: thou wast upon the holy mountain of God; thou hast walked up and down in the midst of the stones of fire. Thou wast perfect in thy ways from the day that thou wast created, till iniquity was found in thee. By the multitude of thy merchandise they have filled the midst of thee with violence, and thou hast sinned: therefore I will cast thee as profane out of the mountain of God: and I will destroy thee, O covering cherub, from the midst of the stones of fire. Thine heart was lifted up because of thy beauty, thou hast corrupted thy wisdom by reason of thy brightness: I will cast thee to the ground, I will lay thee before kings, that they may behold thee" (Ezek. 28:12–17).

Why did Lucifer fall? *"How art thou fallen from heaven, O Lucifer, son of the morning! how art thou cut down to the ground, which didst weaken the nations! For thou hast said* *in thine heart, I will ascend into heaven, I will exalt my throne above the stars of God: I will sit also upon the mount of the congregation, in the sides of the north: I will ascend above the heights of the clouds; I will be like the most High. Yet thou shalt be brought down to hell, to the sides of the pit"* (Isa. 14:12–15).

Can Satan cast himself out? *"And he was casting out a devil, and it was dumb. And it came to pass, when the devil was gone out, the dumb spake; and the people wondered. But some of them said, He casteth out devils through Beelzebub the chief of the devils. And others, tempting him, sought of him a sign from heaven. But he, knowing their thoughts, said unto them, Every kingdom divided against itself is brought to desolation; and a house divided against a house falleth. If Satan also be divided against himself, how shall his kingdom stand? because ye say that I cast out devils through Beelzebub"* (Luke 11:14–18).

Has Satan been permitted into heaven since the fall? *"Now there was a day when the sons of God came to present themselves before the* LORD, *and Satan came also among them"* (Job 1:6).

What is the devil's final outcome? *"And there was war in heaven: Michael and his angels fought against the dragon; and the dragon fought and his angels, And prevailed not; neither was their place found any more in heaven. And the great dragon was cast out, that old serpent, called the Devil, and Satan, which deceiveth the whole world: he was cast out into the earth, and his angels were cast out with him. And I heard a loud voice saying in heaven, Now is come salvation, and strength, and the kingdom of our God, and the power of his Christ: for the accuser of our brethren is cast down, which accused them before our God day and night"* (Rev. 12:7-10).

How will the saints overcome the devil during the Tribulation period? *"And they overcame him by the blood* *of the Lamb, and by the word of their testimony; and they loved not their lives unto the death"* (Rev. 12:11).

Can Christians come against Satan in their own strength? *"Yet Michael the archangel, when contending with the devil he disputed about the body of Moses, durst not bring against him a railing accusation, but said, The Lord rebuke thee"* (Jude 9).

Does Satan have limited access to the believer? *"Hast not thou made an hedge about him, and about his house, and about all that he hath on every side? thou hast blessed the work of his hands, and his substance is increased in the land. But put forth thine hand now, and touch all that he hath, and he will curse thee to thy face. And the* LORD *said unto Satan, Behold, all that he hath is in thy power; only upon himself put not forth thine hand. So Satan went forth from the presence of the* LORD*"* (Job 1:10–12).

Does the devil have power to cause sickness? *"How God anointed Jesus of Nazareth with the Holy Ghost and with power: who went about doing good, and healing all that were oppressed of the devil; for God was with him"* (Acts 10:38).

How did Jesus conquer death? *"Forasmuch then as the children are partakers of flesh and blood, he also himself likewise took part of the same; that through death he might destroy him that had the power of death, that is, the devil"* (Heb. 2:14).

How does Satan attack young leadership in the church? *"Not a novice, lest being lifted up with pride he fall into the condemnation of the devil. Moreover he must have a good report of them which are without; lest he fall into reproach and the snare of the devil"* (1 Tim. 3:6–7).

Can Satan control the very actions of people? *"And supper being ended, the devil having now put into the heart of Judas Iscariot, Simon's son, to betray him"* (John 13:2).

Can Satan personally possess a person? *"And after the sop Satan entered into him. Then said Jesus unto him, That thou doest, do quickly"* (John 13:27).

Will Christians suffer direct persecution from Satan? *"Fear none of those things which thou shalt suffer: behold, the devil shall cast some of you into prison, that ye may be tried; and ye shall have tribulation ten days: be thou faithful unto death, and I will give thee a crown of life"* (Rev. 2:10).

Can Satan hinder the believer from doing the work of God? *"Wherefore we would have come unto you, even I Paul, once and again; but Satan hindered us"* (1 Thess. 2:18).

Will Satan be bound? *"And I saw an angel come down from heaven, having the key of the bottomless pit and a great chain in his hand. And he laid hold on the dragon, that old serpent, which is the Devil, and Satan, and bound him a thousand years, And cast him into the bottomless pit, and shut him up, and set a seal upon him, that he should deceive the nations no more, till the thousand years should be fulfilled: and after that he must be loosed a little season"* (Rev. 20:1–3).

What will the end ultimately be for the devil? *"And the devil that deceived them was cast into the lake of fire and brimstone, where the beast and the false prophet are, and shall be tormented day and night for ever and ever"* (Rev. 20:10).

Is Christ capable of destroying the work of Satan? *"He that committeth sin is of the devil; for the devil sinneth from the beginning. For this purpose the Son of God was manifested, that he might destroy the works of the devil"* (1 John 3:8).

How did Christ destroy sin in a believer's life? *"And you, being dead in your sins and the uncircumcision of your flesh, hath he quickened together with him, having forgiven you all trespasses; Blotting out the handwriting of ordinances* *that was against us, which was contrary to us, and took it out of the way, nailing it to his cross; And having spoiled principalities and powers, he made a shew of them openly, triumphing over them in it"* (Col. 2:13–15).

"Forasmuch then as the children are partakers of flesh and blood, he also himself likewise took part of the same; that through death he might destroy him that had the power of death, that is, the devil; And deliver them who through fear of death were all their lifetime subject to bondage" (Heb. 2:14–15).

Are Christians free? *"To open their eyes, and to turn them from darkness to light, and from the power of Satan unto God, that they may receive forgiveness of sins, and inheritance among them which are sanctified by faith that is in me"* (Acts 26:18).

Why does the devil try to blind the unbeliever? *"In whom the god of this world hath blinded the minds of them which believe not, lest the light of the glorious gospel of Christ, who is the image of God, should shine unto them"* (2 Cor. 4:4).

Are Christians made alive? *"And you hath he quickened, who were dead in trespasses and sins; Wherein in time past ye walked according to the course of this world, according to the prince of the power of the air, the spirit that now worketh in the children of disobedience: Among whom also we all had our conversation in times past in the lusts of our flesh, fulfilling the desires of the flesh and of the mind; and were by nature the children of wrath, even as others"* (Eph. 2:1–3).

Do Christians have power over darkness? *"Who hath delivered us from the power of darkness, and hath translated us into the kingdom of his dear Son"* (Col. 1:13).

Are Christians redeemed? *"In whom we have redemption through his blood, even the forgiveness of sins"* (Col.

1:14).

Must a Christian resist the devil? *"Submit yourselves therefore to God. Resist the devil, and he will flee from you"* (Jam. 4:7).

Must a Christian be sober and vigilant? *"Be sober, be vigilant; because your adversary the devil, as a roaring lion, walketh about, seeking whom he may devour"* (1 Pet. 5:8).

Should a Christian be strong in the Lord? *"Finally, my brethren, be strong in the Lord, and in the power of his might"* (Eph. 6:10).

Is Christ going to crush the devil? *"And the God of peace shall bruise Satan under your feet shortly. The grace of our Lord Jesus Christ be with you. Amen"* (Rom. 16:20).

Should a Christian fear the devil? *"For God hath not given us the spirit of fear; but of power, and of love, and of a sound mind"* (2 Tim. 1:7).

Should we trust a Satanist? *"Ye are of your father the devil, and the lusts of your father ye will do. He was a murderer from the beginning, and abode not in the truth, because there is no truth in him. When he speaketh a lie, he speaketh of his own: for he is a liar, and the father of it"* (John 8:44).

Is it important to forgive? *"To whom ye forgive any thing, I forgive also: for if I forgave any thing, to whom I forgave it, for your sakes forgave I it in the person of Christ; Lest Satan should get an advantage of us: for we are not ignorant of his devices"* (2 Cor. 2:10–11).

Is pride a dangerous foe of the Christian? *"Not a novice, lest being lifted up with pride he fall into the condemnation of the devil"* (1 Tim. 3:6).

Is anger a popular tool against unbelievers? *"Be ye angry, and sin not: let not the sun go down upon your wrath: Neither give place to the devil"* (Eph. 4:26–27).

Can a Christian be oppressed by Satan and why? *"And lest I should be exalted above measure through the abun-*

dance of the revelations, there was given to me a thorn in the flesh, the messenger of Satan to buffet me, lest I should be exalted above measure. For this thing I besought the Lord thrice, that it might depart from me. And he said unto me, My grace is sufficient for thee: for my strength is made perfect in weakness. Most gladly therefore will I rather glory in my infirmities, that the power of Christ may rest upon me. Therefore I take pleasure in infirmities, in reproaches, in necessities, in persecutions, in distresses for Christ's sake: for when I am weak, then am I strong" (2 Cor. 12:7–10).

Can possession occur in children? *"And he asked his father, How long is it ago since this came unto him? And he said, Of a child"* (Mark 9:21).

Is the Christian in battle? *"For though we walk in the flesh, we do not war after the flesh: (For the weapons of our warfare are not carnal, but mighty through God to the pulling down of strongholds)"* (2 Cor. 10:3–4).

Can Christians have the power to take prisoners? *"Casting down imaginations, and every high thing that exalteth itself against the knowledge of God, and bringing into captivity every thought to the obedience of Christ"* (2 Cor. 10:5).

What happens if you do not specifically cast demons into the pit? *"When the unclean spirit is gone out of a man, he walketh through dry places, seeking rest; and finding none, he saith, I will return unto my house whence I came out"* (Luke 11:24).

What happens when a person who was possessed decides to turn over a new leaf without asking Christ to be their Savior? *"And when he cometh, he findeth it swept and garnished. Then goeth he, and taketh to him seven other spirits more wicked than himself; and they enter in, and dwell there: and the last state of that man is worse than the first"* (Luke 11:25–26).

Will Christ protect the believer? *". . . but he that is begotten of God keepeth himself, and that wicked one toucheth him not"* (1 John 5:18).

Does Satan have power to work miracles? *"For there shall arise false Christs, and false prophets, and shall shew great signs and wonders; insomuch that, if it were possible, they shall deceive the very elect. Behold, I have told you before"* (Matt. 24:24–25).

What is the Christian's reward for battle scars? *"Blessed is the man that endureth temptation: for when he is tried, he shall receive the crown of life, which the Lord hath promised to them that love him"* (Jam. 1:12).

Are we to consult Christ and not the occult? *"Thus saith the LORD, the Holy One of Israel, and his Maker, Ask me of things to come concerning my sons, and concerning the work of my hands command ye me. I have made the earth, and created man upon it: I, even my hands, have stretched out the heavens, and all their host have I commanded. I have raised him up in righteousness, and I will direct all his ways: he shall build my city, and he shall let go my captives, not for price nor reward, saith the LORD of hosts"* (Isa. 45:11–13). NOTE: Should a person pay per-visit for information that is supposed to come directly from God? *"Not for price nor reward"* (vs. 13).

Can a person be of the devil yet be very like a Christian? *"Having a form of godliness, but denying the power thereof: from such turn away"* (2 Tim. 3:5).

Who is of the spirit of the Antichrist? *"And every spirit that confesseth not that Jesus Christ is come in the flesh is not of God: and this is that spirit of antichrist, whereof ye have heard that it should come; and even now already is it in the world"* (1 John 4:3). NOTE: Jesus was God who became man, not man who became God.

Does Satan have the power on earth to make one rich

and famous if they worship him? *"Again, the devil taketh him up into an exceeding high mountain, and sheweth him all the kingdoms of the world, and the glory of them; And saith unto him, All these things will I give thee, if thou wilt fall down and worship me"* (Matt. 4:8–9). NOTE: *"For what is a man profited, if he shall gain the whole world, and lose his own soul? or what shall a man give in exchange for his soul?"* (Matt. 16:26).

Can the devil use the name of Jesus to deceive people? Yes. *"For if he that cometh preacheth another Jesus, whom we have not preached, or if ye receive another spirit, which ye have not received, or another gospel, which ye have not accepted, ye might well bear with him"* (2 Cor. 11:4). NOTE: Mormons have another Jesus; the occultist have another Jesus—but not *the* Jesus as taught in the Word.

Can a demon acknowledge Jesus as the Son of God? *"And cried with a loud voice, and said, What have I to do with thee, Jesus, thou Son of the most high God? I adjure thee by God, that thou torment me not"* (Mark 5:7).

"And there was in their synagogue a man with an unclean spirit; and he cried out, Saying, Let us alone; what have we to do with thee, thou Jesus of Nazareth? art thou come to destroy us? I know thee who thou art, the Holy One of God" (Mark 1:23–24). NOTE: They even acknowledged Him as the Son of God, therefore they know who He is. However, there is a big difference in knowing someone and submitting to that person.

Will Jesus come back again as a man? No. *"And Jesus answering them began to say, Take heed lest any man deceive you: For many shall come in my name, saying, I am Christ; and shall deceive many"* (Mark 13:5–6).

Are the devil's workers outwardly vicious? No. *"Beware of false prophets, which come to you in sheep's clothing, but inwardly they are ravening wolves"* (Matt. 7:15).

How can you discern a false prophet? *"Ye shall know them by their fruits. Do men gather grapes of thorns, or figs of thistles? Even so every good tree bringeth forth good fruit; but a corrupt tree bringeth forth evil fruit. A good tree cannot bring forth evil fruit, neither can a corrupt tree bring forth good fruit. Every tree that bringeth not forth good fruit is hewn down, and cast into the fire. Wherefore by their fruits ye shall know them"* (Matt. 7:16–20). NOTE: Make sure you inspect all the fruit, not just a few that look good. Satan's fruits are not always easily detected.

Can a worker of Satan prophesy in Jesus' name? *"Many will say to me in that day, Lord, Lord, have we not prophesied in thy name? . . ."* (Matt. 7:22).

Can they cast out devils? *". . . and in thy name have cast out devils? . . ."* (Matt 7:22). NOTE: Jesus said a devil cannot cast out a devil and this is not a contradiction. A demon cannot cast another demon into the pit; however, a demon will leave at the request of another demon. The purpose is this: when a demon is cast out by another demon-possessed person, the victim is then in bondage to the one who cast it out. When a Christian casts out a demon, the victim is totally in bondage to Jesus Christ, not the Christian involved in the exorcism.

Can a follower of Satan work miracles in Jesus' name? *". . . and in thy name done many wonderful works?"* (Matt. 7:22). NOTE: Remember that the works are done for only one purpose, and that is to deceive.

Because a person's dreams come true, does that mean a Christian should follow them? *"If there arise among you a prophet, or a dreamer of dreams, and giveth thee a sign or a wonder, And the sign or the wonder come to pass, whereof he spake unto thee, saying, Let us go after other gods, which thou hast not known, and let us serve them; Thou shalt not hearken unto the words of that prophet, or that dreamer of* *dreams: for the* LORD *your God proveth you, to know whether ye love the* LORD *your God with all your heart and with all your soul. Ye shall walk after the* LORD *your God, and fear him, and keep his commandments, and obey his voice, and ye shall serve him, and cleave unto him"* (Deut. 13:1–4). NOTE: Edgar Cayce was known as the "sleeping prophet."

What was the penalty for this crime against God? *"And that prophet, or that dreamer of dreams, shall be put to death; because he hath spoken to turn you away from the* LORD *your God . . . But thou shalt surely kill him; thine hand shall be first upon him to put him to death, and afterwards the hand of all the people. And thou shalt stone him with stones, that he die; because he hath sought to thrust thee away from the* LORD *thy God, which brought thee out of the land of Egypt, from the house of bondage"* (Deut. 13:5, 9–10).

What is the purpose of these dreams and visions? *". . . Because he hath spoken to turn you away from the* LORD *your God . . . to thrust thee out of the way which the* LORD *thy God commanded thee to walk in. So shalt thou put the evil away from the midst of thee"* (Deut. 13:5).

Should a person remain loyal to family members who encourage you to serve other gods? *"If thy brother, the son of thy mother, or thy son, or thy daughter, or the wife of thy bosom, or thy friend, which is as thine own soul, entice thee secretly, saying, Let us go and serve other gods, which thou hast not known, thou, nor thy fathers. . . . Thou shalt not consent unto him, nor hearken unto him; neither shall thine eye pity him, neither shalt thou spare, neither shalt thou conceal him"* (Deut. 13:6, 8).

Should a Christian read the horoscopes? *"Thou art wearied in the multitude of thy counsels. Let now the astrologers, the stargazers, the monthly prognosticators, stand up, and save thee from these things that shall come upon thee. Behold, they shall be as stubble; the fire shall burn them;*

they shall not deliver themselves from the power of the flame: there shall not be a coal to warm at, nor fire to sit before it" (Isa. 47:13–14).

Can we rely on the answers given by a devil worshipper? *"Ye are of your father the devil, and the lusts of your father ye will do. He was a murderer from the beginning, and abode not in the truth, because there is no truth in him. When he speaketh a lie, he speaketh of his own: for he is a liar, and the father of it"* (John 8:44). NOTE: Christians believe telling the truth pleases God. A Satanist believes that by lying they obey their god.

Are Satanists supposed to perform murder? See John 8:44. They must obey their father, who was a murderer "from the beginning."

With the rise of suicides, could some be blamed on demon possession? *"And ofttimes it hath cast him into the fire, and into the waters, to destroy him: but if thou canst do any thing, have compassion on us, and help us"* (Mark 9:22). NOTE: The purpose for being thrown into the water and fire was to kill him. This boy was not suicidal by his own will, not suffering from severe depression. (In Mark 5:13 swine were destroyed.)

How does a Christian deal with this particular demon? *"And he said unto them, This kind can come forth by nothing, but by prayer and fasting"* (Mark 9:29).

Is a person demon-possessed if he enjoys inflicting pain on others or himself? *"And always, night and day, he was in the mountains, and in the tombs, crying, and cutting himself with stones"* (Mark 5:5). NOTE: There are those who enjoy cutting themselves, burning their skin with cigarettes, attending slam dances, etc. A doctor does not make a diagnosis by only one symptom; they run a series of tests. So not everyone that hurts himself is demon possessed.

People sell their souls to the devil in return for plea-

sure, but are all demon-possessed people happy? *"And always, night and day, he was in the mountains, and in the tombs, crying, and cutting himself with stones"* (Mark 5:5). NOTE: This man probably would be diagnosed today as suffering from severe anxiety. As you see the worship of demons more and more in America, you also find a greater number of young people in mental wards. (Again, not every case is one of demon-possession.)

NEW AGE

What does the Scripture say about astrology? *"Thou art wearied in the multitude of thy counsels. Let now the astrologers, the stargazers, the monthly prognosticators, stand up, and save thee from these things that shall come upon thee. Behold, they shall be as stubble; the fire shall burn them; they shall not deliver themselves from the power of the flame: there shall not be a coal to warm at, nor fire to sit before it"* (Isa. 47:13–14).

Concerning reincarnation, the New Age teaches that man will become as gods. Is this true? *"For God doth know that in the day ye eat thereof, then your eyes shall be opened, and ye shall be as gods, knowing good and evil"* (Gen. 3:5).

Should a person consult channellers? (Channelling is a New Age term for possession. People like Shirley MacLaine and Linda Evans advocate going to channellers who speak by "spirit guides.") *"Then said Saul unto his servants, Seek me a woman that hath a familiar spirit, that I may go to her, and enquire of her. And his servants said to him, Behold, there is a woman that hath a familiar spirit at Endor. And Saul disguised himself, and put on other raiment, and he went, and two men with him, and they came to the woman by night: and he said, I pray thee, divine unto me by the familiar spirit, and bring me him up, whom I shall name unto thee"* (1 Sam.

28:7–8). NOTE: When Saul was right with God, he was against such things.

Can a channeller say good things of Christians? Can they tell the future? *"And it came to pass, as we went to prayer, a certain damsel possessed with a spirit of divination met us, which brought her masters much gain by soothsaying"* (Acts 16:16). NOTE: Paul spoke to the spirit, not the woman. *"And this did she many days. But Paul, being grieved, turned and said to the spirit, I command thee in the name of Jesus Christ to come out of her. And he came out the same hour"* (vs. 18).

Should your children watch cartoons with wizards? *"Regard not them that have familiar spirits, neither seek after wizards, to be defiled by them: I am the LORD your God"* (Lev. 19:31).

Does God tolerate or endorse a witch when he claims to be a Christian? *"A man also or woman that hath a familiar spirit, or that is a wizard, shall surely be put to death: they shall stone them with stones: their blood shall be upon them"* (Lev. 20:27). NOTE: God is "the same yesterday, today, and forever."

What about tarot cards, Ouija boards, crystal balls, and other occultic tools? *"If there arise among you a prophet, or a dreamer of dreams, and giveth thee a sign or a wonder, And the sign or the wonder come to pass, whereof he spake unto thee, saying, Let us go after other gods, which thou hast not known, and let us serve them; Thou shalt not hearken unto the words of that prophet, or that dreamer of dreams: for the LORD your God proveth you, to know whether ye love the LORD your God with all your heart and with all your soul"* (Deut. 13:1–3). NOTE: People who use the devil's tools will never lead you to a saving knowledge of God.

Should Christians run to places where people claimed Jesus or Mary have appeared? *"Then if any man shall say* *unto you, Lo, here is Christ, or there; believe it not. For there shall arise false Christs, and false prophets, and shall shew great signs and wonders; insomuch that, if it were possible, they shall deceive the very elect. Behold, I have told you before"* (Matt. 24:23–25).

How will Christ appear when He comes again? *"For as the lightning cometh out of the east, and shineth even unto the west; so shall also the coming of the Son of man be"* (Matt. 24:27). NOTE: He will not appear on screens and walls; He will come in glory.

What is the danger in following the New Age teaching that man will become as a god? *"Who changed the truth of God into a lie, and worshipped and served the creature more than the Creator, who is blessed for ever. Amen"* (Rom. 1:25). NOTE: Romans 1:26–31 tells of people who made themselves to be as God.

Should a person try to contact those who are dead? *"And when they shall say unto you, Seek unto them that have familiar spirits, and unto wizards that peep, and that mutter: should not a people seek unto their God? for the living to the dead?"* (Isa. 8:19). NOTE: Our God is a living God; therefore, those who seek the dead must go to the god of death rather than the God of the Living.

"There shall not be found among you any one that maketh his son or his daughter to pass through the fire, or that useth divination, or an observer of times, or an enchanter, or a witch, Or a charmer, or a consulter with familiar spirits, or a wizard, or a necromancer. For all that do these things are an abomination unto the LORD: and because of these abominations the LORD thy God doth drive them out from before thee" (Deut. 18:10–12).

NOTE PROBLEM: *"And he made his son pass through the fire, and observed times, and used enchantments, and dealt with familiar spirits and wizards: he wrought much wicked-*

ness in the sight of the LORD, to provoke him to anger" (2 Kings 21:6).

NOTE PENALTY: *"Because Manasseh king of Judah hath done these abominations, and hath done wickedly above all that the Amorites did, which were before him, and hath made Judah also to sin with his idols: Therefore thus saith the LORD God of Israel, Behold, I am bringing such evil upon Jerusalem and Judah, that whosoever heareth of it, both his ears shall tingle"* (2 Kings 21:11–12).

Can Satan's disciples perform miracles? *"Then Pharaoh also called the wise men and the sorcerers: now the magicians of Egypt, they also did in like manner with their enchantments. For they cast down every man his rod, and they became serpents: but Aaron's rod swallowed up their rods"* (Exod. 7:11–12). NOTE: Miracles are not always a sign from the Lord.

What is the purpose of a sorcerer? To turn a man's heart from God? *"And when they had gone through the isle unto Paphos, they found a certain sorcerer, a false prophet, a Jew, whose name was Barjesus: Which was with the deputy of the country, Sergius Paulus, a prudent man; who called for Barnabas and Saul, and desired to hear the word of God. But Elymas the sorcerer (for so is his name by interpretation) withstood them, seeking to turn away the deputy from the faith. Then Saul, (who also is called Paul,) filled with the Holy Ghost, set his eyes on him, And said, O full of all subtilty and all mischief, thou child of the devil, thou enemy of all righteousness, wilt thou not cease to pervert the right ways of the Lord?"* (Acts 13:6–10).

Should a person who claims to be a Christian follow mediums and wizards? *"Regard not them that have familiar spirits, neither seek after wizards, to be defiled by them: I am the LORD your God. . . . And the soul that turneth after such as have familiar spirits, and after wizards, to go a* *whoring after them, I will even set my face against that soul, and will cut him off from among his people"* (Lev. 19:31; 20:6).

Will people in the latter days turn to the Lord for guidance? *"Now the Spirit speaketh expressly, that in the latter times some shall depart from the faith, giving heed to seducing spirits, and doctrines of devils"* (1 Tim. 4:1).

Can Christians have victory over these spirits? *"Now thanks be unto God, which always causeth us to triumph in Christ, and maketh manifest the savour of his knowledge by us in every place"* (2 Cor. 2:14).

Should we as Christians be ignorant of Satan's devices? *"Lest Satan should get an advantage of us: for we are not ignorant of his devices"* (2 Cor. 2:11).

How do Christians overcome the devil? *"And they overcame him by the blood of the Lamb, and by the word of their testimony; and they loved not their lives unto the death"* (Rev. 12:11).

What does the Bible say about the dragon? *"And the great dragon was cast out, that old serpent, called the Devil, and Satan, which deceiveth the whole world: he was cast out into the earth, and his angels were cast out with him"* (Rev. 12:9).

What was Satan like before the fall? *"Son of man, take up a lamentation upon the king of Tyrus, and say unto him, Thus saith the Lord GOD; Thou sealest up the sum, full of wisdom, and perfect in beauty"* (Ezek. 28:12).

Can we rebuke the devil in our own strength? *"Yet Michael the archangel, when contending with the devil he disputed about the body of Moses, durst not bring against him a railing accusation, but said, The Lord rebuke thee"* (Jude 9).

What about guardian angels (angels that minister to saints)? *"Are they not all ministering spirits, sent forth to* *minister for them who shall be heirs of salvation?"* (Heb. 1:14).

Can the devil reward his followers? *"And the devil, taking him up into an high mountain, shewed unto him all the kingdoms of the world in a moment of time. And the devil said unto him, All this power will I give thee, and the glory of them: for that is delivered unto me; and to whomsoever I will I give it"* (Luke 4:5–6). NOTE: *"For what is a man profited, if he shall gain the whole world, and lose his own soul? or what shall a man give in exchange for his soul?"* (Matt. 16:26).

Do those who follow astrology disobey the commands of the Lord? *"And they left all the commandments of the* LORD *their God, and made them molten images, even two calves, and made a grove, and worshipped all the host of heaven, and served Baal. And they caused their sons and their daughters to pass through the fire, and used divination and enchantments, and sold themselves to do evil in the sight of the* LORD, *to provoke him to anger"* (2 Kings 17:16–17). NOTE: It started with astrology and ended with human sacrifice.

What should be done with former objects of astrology and witchcraft? *"And the king commanded Hilkiah the high priest, and the priests of the second order, and the keepers of the door, to bring forth out of the temple of the* LORD *all the vessels that were made for Baal, and for the grove, and for all the host of heaven: and he burned them without Jerusalem in the fields of Kidron, and carried the ashes of them unto Bethel"* (2 Kings 23:4).

Did God tolerate astrology in Old Testament times? *"If there be found among you, within any of thy gates which the* LORD *thy God giveth thee, man or woman, that hath wrought wickedness in the sight of the* LORD *thy God, in transgressing his covenant, And hath gone and served other gods,* *and worshipped them, either the sun, or moon, or any of the host of heaven, which I have not commanded; And it be told thee, and thou hast heard of it, and enquired diligently, and, behold, it be true, and the thing certain, that such abomination is wrought in Israel: Then shalt thou bring forth that man or that woman, which have committed that wicked thing, unto thy gates, even that man or that woman, and shalt stone them with stones, till they die"* (Deut. 17:2–5).

Should Christians have graven images in their homes (i.e., zodiac signs, favorite rock albums, etc.)? *"Thou shalt not make thee any graven image, or any likeness of any thing that is in heaven above, or that is in the earth beneath, or that is in the waters beneath the earth"* (Deut. 5:8).

Is it God's will for us to know all about the future? *"And he said unto them, It is not for you to know the times or the seasons, which the Father hath put in his own power. But ye shall receive power, after that the Holy Ghost is come upon you: and ye shall be witnesses unto me both in Jerusalem, and in all Judea, and in Samaria, and unto the uttermost part of the earth"* (Acts 1:7–8).

Should a Christian practice and teach reading tea leaves, palm reading, tarot cards, witching for water, etc.? *"When thou art come into the land which the LORD thy God giveth thee, thou shalt not learn to do after the abominations of those nations. There shall not be found among you any one that maketh his son or his daughter to pass through the fire, or that useth divination, or an observer of times, or an enchanter, or a witch, Or a charmer, or a consulter with familiar spirits, or a wizard, or a necromancer. For all that do these things are an abomination unto the LORD: and because of these abominations the LORD thy God doth drive them out from before thee"* (Deut. 18:9–12).

What about reincarnation? *"And as it is appointed unto men once to die, but after this the judgment"* (Heb. 9:27).

Notes

Chapter One—God Will Not Protect Children . . .

Chapter Two—That Bad Witches and Good Witches . . .
1. Berit Kjos, *Your Child and the New Age* (Victor Books, 1990), p. 168.
2. Rosemary Ellen Guiley, *Encyclopedia of Witches & Witchcraft* (Facts on File, 1989), p. 214
3. *Associated Press, January 26, 1991.*

Chapter Three—That Witches in White Magic and . . .
1. Richard Cavendish, *Man, Myth, and Magic*, Vol. II (Marshall Cavendish Co., Long Island, NY, 1983) p. 3018.

Chapter Four—That Witches Actively Proselytize Children
1. Suzanne Perney, "Trouble Brewing in Salem," *Boston Herald's Sunday People* (Boston, Mass.), October 27, 1991, p. 6.
2. Johanna Michaelsen, *Like Lambs to the Slaughter* (Harvest House Publishers, Eugene, Ore., 1989), p. 198.
3. Texe Marrs, *Flashpoint*, June 1992.
4. Paddy Slade, *Encyclopedia of White Magic* (Mallard Press, New York).
5. Erica Jong, *Witches* (Harry N. Abrams, New York, 1981), p. 101.
6. T.C. Lethbridge, *Witches*, First Edition (Citadel Press, New York, 1968), pp. 13–14.
7. Rosemary Ellen Guiley, *Encyclopedia of Witches and Witchcraft* (Facts on File, 1989), p. 18.
8. Johanna Michaelsen, *Like Lambs to the Slaughter*, p. 200.

Chapter Five—Witches and Satanists Have Some Things . . .
1. Paddy Slade, *Encyclopedia of White Magic*. See index.
2. Ibid.
3. Suzanne Perney, "Trouble Brewing in Salem," *Boston Herald's Sunday People*, October 27, 1991, p. 8.
4. Johanna Michaelsen, *Like Lambs to the Slaughter*, p. 63.
5. Rosemary Ellen Guiley, *Encyclopedia of Witches & Witchcraft*, p. 17.
6. Sybil Leek, *Moon Signs* (Berkley Publishing Group, New York City, 1977), inside cover.
7. Ibid., p. 197.
8. *Premium Channels TV Blueprint*, New York, October 1991, p. 7.
9. Suzy Parker, USA Today, Gallup poll.

Chapter Six—Witches and Satanists Use the Media . . .
1. *U.S. Chaplain's Manual.*
3. Ibid.
3. Suzanne Perney, "Trouble Brewing in Salem," *Boston Herald's Sunday People*, October 27, 1991, p. 9.
4. Ibid.
5. Ibid.

Chapter Seven—Satan Is "Trolling" for Souls
1. Wade Baskin, *Dictionary of Satanism* (Philosophical Library, New York, 1972), p. 323.
2. Richard Cavendish, *Man, Myth, and Magic,* Vol. 11, p. 2889.
3. Ibid.
4. Ibid.

Chapter Eight—Lucifer Is Quite a Charmer

Chapter Nine—Witches Do "Knot" Play Fair
1. Rosemary Ellen Guiley, *Encyclopedia of Witches and Witchcraft*, p. 187.
2. Johanna Michaelsen, *Like Lambs to the Slaughter*, pp. 182–183.

Chapter Ten—Smurfs Are Not "True Blue"
1. Rosemary Ellen Guiley, *Encyclopedia of Witches & Witchcraft*, p. 219.
2. Ibid., p. 218.
3. Ibid., pp. 218–219.

Chapter Eleven—Something Smells a "Little Fishy" . . .
1. Richard Cavendish, *Man, Myth, and Magic*, Vol. 11, p. 1812.
2. Kathryn Paulsen, *The Complete Book of Magic and Witchcraft* (Signet Books, New York, 1970), p. 150.

Chapter Twelve—Turtles Are "Zeroes" Not "Heroes"
1. *USA Today*, Section 2D, March 18, 1991.
2. *USA Today.*
3. *USA Today*, August 31, 1992.
4. Roshi Kapeau, *The Three Pillars of Zen* (Anchor Books, Doubleday, New York, 1980), preface XV.
5. Anne Bancroft, *Zen—Direct Pointing to Reality* (Thames Hudson, New York, 1987), p. 9.
6. Ibid., p. 90.
7. Bobby Herbeck, *Teenage Mutant Ninja Turtles—The Storybook Based*

on the Movie (Random House, New York, 1990), p. 30.

8. Ibid., pp. 29–30.

9. Deborah Rozman, *Meditating with Children* (University of the Trees Press, Cal., 1975), inside cover.

10. Ibid., p. 58.

11. Samuel Silverstein, *Child Spirit* (Bear and Co., Santa Fe, NM, 1991).

12. John Gentile, *Teenage Mutant Ninja Turtles Special Comic Book,* "Doomsday Hassle in Banshee Castle" (Archie Comic Publications, New York, 1993).

13. Samuel Silverstein, *Child Spirit*, p. 72.

14. John Gentile, *Teenage Mutant Ninja Turtles Special Comic Book,* "Doomsday Hassle in Banshee Castle."

Chapter Thirteen—Bart Simpson Has His Own Values System

Chapter Fourteen—"He's Man" and "She's God"

1. David Alexander, *Humanist Magazine*, "Gene Roddenberry," March–April 1991, p. 5.

2. Johanna Michaelsen, *Like Lambs to the Slaughter*, p. 222.

3. Ibid., p. 222.

Appendix One—Ecology or Theology

1. Richard Ostling, *Time*, "When God Was a Woman," May 6, 1991, p. 73.

2. *The Charlotte Observer*, "Witches, Warlocks—Meeting in Mexico to Put a Hex on City's Pollution," March 7, 1993.

Appendix Two—Beauty and the Beast

1. Mme. Le Prince de Beaumont, *Beauty and the Beast* (The Limited Edition Club, New York, 1949), pp. 5–6.

Appendix Three—Barney

1. Berit Kjos, *Your Child and the New Age*, p. 167.

2. Samuel Silverstein, *Child Spirit*, p. 26.

3. Ibid., back cover.

4. *Operation Vampire Killer 2000* (American Citizens and Lawman Association, Phoenix, Ariz., 1992), p. 23.

5. Samuel Silverstein, *Child Spirit*, p. 3.

Appendix Four—Situation Ethics and Those Who Have None

1. Rosemary Ellen Guiley, *Encyclopedia of Witches & Witchcraft*, p. 105.

Appendix Five—Bereavement and Braindead
1. *Newsweek*, October 11, 1993.

Appendix Six—Yin and Yang Made Plain
1. Bob Larson, *Larson's Book of Cults* (Tyndale House Publishers, Inc., Wheaton, Ill., 1983), p. 98.
2. Ibid., p. 98.
3. William B. Eerdman, *Eerdman's Handbook to the World's Religions* (Wm. B. Eerdman's Publishing Co., Grand Rapids, Mich., 1982), p. 435.

Notes

I don't get most of the book.

About the Author

David Benoit (Ben-wah) was born March 14, 1955, and grew up in Louisiana. He accepted Christ as Savior in 1972 after a rebellious teenage life had led him to reform school. In 1973 he enrolled in Liberty University, graduating in 1978.

In June of 1984, David was led of the Lord to establish Glory Ministries. The emphasis of Glory Ministries is exposing the truth about the damaging effects of rock music on society, the only solution being regeneration by Jesus Christ.

Mr. Benoit's vast knowledge of the occult and New Age has now led him into a full-time ministry of exposing the subtleties of Satan's devices.

David has appeared on hundreds of local radio and television talk shows across the country, the most notable including Trinity Broadcasting Network (TBN), Inspirational Network, Family Broadcasting Network, Moody Broadcasting Network, KGO radio (San Francisco), WGST radio (Atlanta), WWWE radio (Cleveland), Point of View (Dallas, Texas), Dr. D. James Kennedy's nationally televised program, and Southwest Radio Church.

He is a regular speaker in churches as well as Christian school conventions and family seminars. Mr. Benoit has the very rare ability to communicate his message to young people, as well as to their parents. David seeks for his ministry to assist the local fundamental Bible-believing churches of America and overseas in evangelism outreach and subsequent church growth.

Speaking engagements can be arranged by Hearthstone Publishing, c/o Karin Ferguson, P.O. Box 1144, Oklahoma City, OK 73101, or at (405) 235-5396.

Television and radio interviews can be scheduled through C.L.A.S.S. at (619) 471-1722.

Also by David Benoit

14 Things Witches Hope Parents Never Find Out
ISBN 1-879366-76-2   2 audio tapes

Occult Tendencies in Rock Music
ISBN 1-879366-77-0   Video

Violence in Rock Music
ISBN 1-879366-78-9   Video

When God Calls the New World to Order
ISBN 1-879366-79-7   Video

Also Available from Hearthstone Publishing

The Revived Roman Empire and the Beast of the Apocalypse
N.W. Hutchings
ISBN 1-879366-31-2   150 pages

Vladimir Zhirinovsky: The Man Who Would Be Gog
Scot Overbey
ISBN 1-879366-74-6   150 pages

Vladimir Zhirinovsky and the Last Dash to the South
Scot Overbey and Mark Hitchcock
ISBN 1-879366-73-8   Video

Why I Still Believe These Are the Last Days
ISBN 1-879366-38-X   250 pages

Footprints and the Stones of Time
Dr. Carl Baugh and Dr. Clifford Wilson
ISBN 1-879366-17-7   150 pages—Illustrated

Why So Many Churches?
N.W. Hutchings
ISBN 1-879366-28-2   200 pages

Petra In History and Prophecy
N.W. Hutchings
ISBN 1-879366-11-8   160 pages—Illustrated

For ordering information, call 1-800-652-1144.